MW01657131

GEORGEGODDAMMITSTOPTHAT

Confessions of a 1950's Free-Range Child

George Young

Dedication

This book is a tribute to the magnificent souls who've crafted, chiseled, sparked, nudged, and twisted me into the wondrous creature you see before you today. To the standout heroes: your impact was cosmic! And to those mischievous troublemakers, thanks for keeping life spicy.

Contents

INTRODUCTION

GEORGEGODDAMMITSTOPTHAT

Growing up in a small Hoosier town during the 1950s feels like a stroke of luck. Life was laid-back, and crime was a rarity. Our doors remained unlocked. It wasn't exactly an Andy of Mayberry scenario, but it allowed us to thrive as free-range children in an environment that fostered independence.

During my early years, I basked in the sole attention lavished upon me as an only child, thoroughly indulged by my parents and grandparents. Then, seemingly out of nowhere, my mother blessed me with two siblings within thirteen months.

Initially, I found it very intriguing until reality struck that they were neither entertaining nor self-sufficient—they craved my mother's undivided attention. Suddenly, I was no longer the focal point of her world. This marked the start of my journey as a child with ample freedom, typical of the 1950s. Our neighborhood was friendly and safe, granting me the freedom I craved. After my siblings appeared, I was encouraged to spend as much time outdoors as possible, exploring the treasures of our neighborhood. The only significant rule I recall was "Don't Slam the Door" to avoid disturbing the babies. My boundaries were loose, and I constantly tested them on my tricycle and, later, my bike.

My mother, the enforcer of rules and disciplinarian in our family transformed into a more irritable figure as her responsibilities multiplied after the arrival of my siblings and my own resistance to the newfound lack of attention.

My behavior spiraled downward, and my mother's disciplinary methods became harsher, resorting to swats with whatever object was close at hand: a flyswatter, a wooden spoon, or even a shoe.

It wasn't until I turned nine that I realized my full name wasn't really "GEORGEGODDAMMITSTOPTHAT." I can still hear my mother yelling that many times a day for absolutely no reason.

I vividly remember kindergarten, housed in a neighbor's home two blocks away. With two babies to manage, my mother allowed me to walk alone since there were no major streets to cross—a significant expansion of my world. It all went off without a hitch until one day; I arrived at Mrs. Cooper's house for class wearing only one shoe. After a phone call to my mother, Mrs. Cooper was assured that I indeed left home wearing both shoes. The shoe was located not far away. This was only one of the first of my Free-Range life experiences.

As first grade approached, I lived half a mile from school with major streets to navigate. My kindergarten experiences prepared me well, and I was eager to explore. My path home wasn't always direct; it resembled a 'Family Circus' cartoon as I meandered through yards, collecting intriguing objects. I learned to vary my route to avoid a bully, honing my navigation skills.

Scientists have discovered that the male adolescent brain isn't fully developed until twenty-five. I have included a few stories from my early adulthood proving this to be true.

Reflecting on my childhood, it's akin to the movie 'Stand by Me' without the discovery of a corpse. I didn't have Ben E King's cool soundtrack, but the cicadas sang their tunes in the sweltering Hoosier summers. Looking back, I feel like Rob Reiner could have improved his film if he had followed my childhood adventures. Though perhaps embellished by my septuagenarian mind, these stories remain mine to share.

DePrez House & Dog Rescue

Charles Davis Mansion

When I was a kid in the 1950s, a large three-story Victorian Mansion on Mechanic St was located just around the corner from my early childhood home on Saint Mary Street. Yes, I said mansion. It was huge compared to my home. I walked past this mammoth house every day on the way to school.

We called it the DePrez house because the owners then were Brigadier General D. Wray DePrez and his wife, Virginia. The house was so big that it had live-in servants' quarters with a private staircase. As a kid, I didn't know the house's history, but I have since learned that the DePrez family was the second owner of this house.

The Charles Davis Mansion was built in 1898 by Charles Davis, a furniture manufacturing scion and president of the Davis-Birely Table Company. During the late 1800s & early 1900s, Shelbyville, Indiana's nationally recognized historic district, began to take shape. In the early 1900s,

Shelbyville boasted over twenty furniture manufacturers, and the Davis-Birely Table Company became known internationally. It was recognized as the world's largest exclusive manufacturer of library & parlor tables at the time. After Charles Davis's untimely death in 1911, the home became the family compound in the 1920s for Brigadier General D.W. DePrez, Commanding Officer of the 76th Infantry Brigade of the 38th Division, Indiana National Guard in WW2.

At Christmas time, our family would drive around town at night to see how other people had decorated their houses with lights and such for the season. It was much like the movie 'Christmas Story' except no one had a leg lamp displayed in their front window. The best part of our tour was always seeing how the DePrez house had been professionally decorated that year. Interior decorators from department stores in Indianapolis were commissioned to make the season festive. They always had an elaborate tree prominently displayed in the front window. I especially remember one year the tree was covered in large blue feathers. It was so pretty that we drove around several times with many Ohhs and Awws from the family.

This dog rescue story began innocently one day when a buddy, Wilton, and I were walking down Mechanic Street. We were 7-year-old free-range kids on the way to some adventure for the day when Mrs. DePrez came out on the front porch excitedly, shouting that both her dogs had gotten loose and asked us to help round them up. I remember they had kennels out the back of the house, but I don't know the breed of dogs, only that they were large. Maybe boxers?

We were glad to help. Whatever adventure we had planned could wait. Immediately, we began searching the neighborhood, looking in every alley and backyard. Soon, Wilton and I located both dogs. The dogs were amiable, and we could get them back to their home without difficulty. Mrs. DePrez was so pleased that she invited us in for some refreshments. I think it was homemade lemonade and cookies served by her maid. She also gave us some money as a reward. She was that pleased to have her dogs safely back home. I don't remember how much money she gave us, but it was a king's ransom to Wilton and me. Before this windfall, we would collect pop bottles from wherever we could to return to the stores to buy penny candies.

Wilton and I had money-burning holes in our pockets for weeks. We could buy candy bars daily and soda pop whenever we wanted. No more penny candies for us. It was terrific. We even went to Linne's, the local bakery, and splurged on chocolate eclairs. Then, just as quickly as it happened, our newfound wealth was gone. We should have had a little more restraint. We went back to searching the alleys for pop bottles for spending money.

They say necessity is the mother of invention. Before our big reward, we didn't realize we were poor. Now that we had experienced the sweet life of having lots of cash, stark reality became very difficult. So, we hatched a plot to revisit the scene of our great reward. We knew the odds of the dogs escaping again were very low, so we decided to liberate them from their kennels and take them for a walk.

After we had them gone for a while, we decided to take them back to the front door. We rang the bell, and Mrs. DePrez came to the door. Armed with big smiles, we explained how we found her dogs loose again and knew she must be distraught. She thanked us profusely and dug into her pocketbook again for another vast reward. Eureka, we had indeed revealed the goose that laid golden eggs. After being thanked profusely by an ever-grateful Mrs. DePrez, it was off to Linne's to treat ourselves to something special.

Wilton and I enjoyed our reward money, but it wasn't quite as sweet this time. We bought candy for some friends but didn't divulge our secret benefactor. The money didn't last as long this time since we were sharing, and soon, we found ourselves flat-broke again. Plus, we had this empty feeling deep in our souls.

Wilton decided it was time to make Mrs. DePrez happy again by rescuing her beloved dogs. I was in total agreement. Who doesn't like making old ladies happy? We quietly sneaked into the backyard, opened the kennel gates, and took the pups for a stroll around the block again. The dogs seemed so glad to see us. Helping exercise their pets was a good thing, right? We walked up to the front door with the dogs in tow and were greeted at the door by Mr. DePrez, a.k a. the 'General.' We didn't even have to ring the doorbell. The General was waiting with his crossed arms and scowling like he was ready to court martial guilty soldiers. In a stern voice, he informed us that he had watched us take the dogs from the kennel and knew we had fooled his wife at least once. I don't remember the exact

Brig-Gen D.W. Deprez

words of his lecture, but it was clear Wilton and I had killed the goose that laid the golden eggs.

DePrez's fondness for children was also legendary around town. They were known for having hot cocoa and cookies ready for Christmas carolers. My wife remembers how nice it was on a cold night after singing with her Girl Scout troop. I wonder if Mr. DePrez would have spotted my bad singing and denied me cookies.

Santa Beer and Cheese Snack

Nobody gives you a rule book for being a dad. You are just thrown in the deep end and hope for the best. When my son Derek was in the first grade, he still believed in Santa. At least he didn't let on that he suspected the ruse. I liked doing all the fun things around the Christmas holiday, like setting up the tree, decorating the house, and visiting Santa at the Mall. We started our Christmas Eve traditions, like putting out milk and cookies for Santa when he was a wee tike. We would talk about how hard Santa had to work going around the world bringing toys for all the children. Just keeping eight reindeer flying was a difficult task that kept Santa burning calories. All this work made him extremely hungry, so we had to reward him with 'Milk and Cookies' so he could continue worldwide in one night.

On Christmas morning, Derek would wake up and run to check that Santa had indeed eaten his snack. The night before, I would pour out part of the glass of milk since I was a little lactose intolerant and then eat half of each cookie since I was cookie tolerant. Derek would then sprint to the tree and find Santa had indeed left presents for him. A tradition was established in the Young household.

Being a new parent, I didn't know the dangers of changing family traditions, but I decided to change things when Derek was in the first grade. I talked to Derek about changing the Cookies and Milk routine on Christmas Eve. We talked about how boring it must be to get the same treat house after house. He agreed that Santa would like a change of pace with a savory snack. Derek even speculated that Santa would probably reward him with more and better presents. How cool was it that I just made Christmas more fun? Being a dad was easy.

After reading the book 'Twas the Night Before Christmas, ' it was time to prepare Santa's snack. Derek and I arranged a plate with gouda cheese, Hickory Farm summer sausage, and crackers with a cold can of beer. Derek agreed that that would be a tasty surprise for the jolly fat man in red. Derek didn't like those items, but he knew I had frequently eaten them as an after-dinner snack, so he was sure Santa would also. It was off to bed for him, dreaming of sugar plums dancing in his head. Now, it was time for the parental units to get into action. After several false starts of getting out of bed to check if Santa had been there, he finally went to sleep. We gathered and positioned all the hidden presents from their hiding spots around the tree. I then went to Santa Snack tray, devoured it all, and drank the beer and maybe a couple more from the fridge. I left a few crumbs on the plate and put the crushed beer cans on the plate.

It was time for us to collapse into bed, knowing the little guy would awaken before dawn, ready to get presents. Sure enough, at 5 AM, a little hand was poking me, saying Santa had been here and eaten his snack. It was time to unwrap Christmas presents.

It was a fantastic Christmas holiday; everyone enjoyed their presents. Derek even remarked that Santa had eaten all his snacks this year compared to half-eaten in previous years. Kids notice every little thing and retain odd details. This would surely help the future naughty or nice list that Santa kept. All the holiday debris was disposed of, the tree was taken down, and decorations were put away, ready for the following year. The tiring Christmas holiday ended, and we could move on with everyday life. Wrong!

Fast forward to mid-January, when it was time for our first visit to see Derek's 1st-grade classroom; we already knew his teacher and her husband socially. I played racquetball with him, so I had been getting updates on his academic progress. As we toured the school, we saw where they had recess, lunchroom, gymnasium, etc. It was time to visit his classroom and see his cubby and desk. He was very excited to show us everything. All around the room were posted 'kid stories' the children had written about 'What I did on Christmas holiday.' Some kids went sledding; others visited grandma, and some went to Florida. Nowhere could I find Derek's essay. I asked him if he had written one, and he said: "Yes, it was about Santa." I looked again, thinking maybe I just had missed it. Finally, I approached the teacher and asked what happened to Derek's. She crooked her finger to follow her to her desk, where she opened a drawer, pulled out a folder, and handed us his story.

> SANTA HATE MILK AND COOKIES
> ME AND DADDY MAKE CHEESE AND KRACKERS AND BEER 4 SANTA. SANTA ATE IT ALL. HE KRUSKED BEER CAN ON HEAD. I HEARED HIM BURP. I AM ON HIS NICE LIST NOW.
> DEREK

The teacher looked at us like WTF are you doing to this child? She said she didn't want to embarrass him in front of classmates, so she didn't post it on the blackboard. I tried to explain, but she shook her head and walked away. It didn't help that we got a note sent home that she had to stop Derek from putting his finger in the electric pencil sharpener a few weeks later.

As I said, nobody gives you a rule book when you first become a parent; it's trial and error—lots of errors, at least on my part. The first kid is like making pancakes; the first always turns out weird, and you get better as you make more. Yes, we stopped the beer and cheese for Santa tradition. Santa sent a note explaining that he was now going to AA and wanted cookies and milk.

Fire Station Lifetime Ban

Growing up in the 1950s in a small town gave me many freedoms that aren't possible today. My two small siblings occupied my mother's time; frankly, having me in the house underfoot complicated her life. I was a free-range child who was expected home for mealtimes and when the streetlights came on. I often played outside in the neighborhood, but my buddies and I frequently wandered all over town. We visited the library, swimming pool, and city parks for supervised activities. Well, that was always the plan. Plus, we always said to our mothers when we left the house. Deviations from the plan happened on the spur of the moment and were driven by whatever popped into our heads that day.

The library was a great place on the hottest of days. Indiana summertime always had days when the temperature would be in the 90s with humidity to match. The attraction to the library on days like that wasn't the intellectual pursuits but the fact that our Carnegie library was constructed with lots of marble, keeping the temperatures very low. Air conditioning in those days was non-existent. We would head there to cool off and hang out during the hottest part of the day. They had a kid's section where we could gather and grab some books to pretend to read. A group of young boys gathered was a sure bet for raised voices and arm punching. The librarians were pros at handling this, but it presented another danger for me. Two of our librarians were sisters who were cousins to my grandmother. Not only did they feel free to give me an extra dose of discipline, but they would also relay my behavior to my grandmother when I got out of hand. Still, we continued to seek refuge from the heat and even absorbed some knowledge along the way.

One day, I grabbed my buddy Wilton and told him it was time to skedaddle from the library before we got kicked out. Right across the street was the fire station. This was also a great place to explore. We had been there many times before. The firemen had always welcomed us and were willing to let us explore the station and equipment. They would gladly answer our questions and let us pretend to be firemen. Our little town had few fires, so they seemed bored and liked us. We had previously climbed all over the fire engines wearing firemen hats. Today was different, but no firemen were in sight. I am guessing now with my adult brain that maybe they'd had a rough night with an actual big fire and were upstairs in their bunks catching up on sleep. Back then, we thought the open door meant we had free reign to play as we saw fit.

Fire Station #1- Broadway Street

The imaginations of two eight-year-old boys unsupervised in a fire station might not have been ideal. Since there were two fire engines, we each would pretend to drive our own. A great game of "Let's Pretend" started. In our minds, we had a two-alarm fire that needed our attention (Yes, the firemen taught us some lingo). We had great fun when we got the brilliant idea to take the game up a notch.

On our previous visits, we learned about the various knobs

and buttons in the cab of the engines. We knew the firetrucks always had their sirens blaring when racing to a fire. We decided this would be great fun; Firemen were always happy. We somehow managed to get the headlights on, plus the flashing red lights and sirens for both fire engines. It was spectacular in that small space where they parked the fire engines. It was way more fun than being shushed by some dowdy old librarians. Little did we know how much commotion we had instigated. Firemen began rushing from everywhere, thinking they had a call to respond to. Firemen were sliding down the pole from upstairs and their bunks, putting on their gear and getting ready to take off. They soon discovered it was just two kids playing "Fireman."

That's when the swearing and yelling commenced as they jumped into the trucks to turn off all the switches we had turned on. It was total chaos. We looked at each other in full panic for just a few moments and decided to get out of there. Firemen were chasing Wilton and me out of the building and screaming as we ran as fast as we could up Broadway Street away from the angry firemen. I can still hear them yelling. Let's just say we were banned from the fire station for life. I wonder if our lifetime ban is still in effect.

Car Wreck World Record

I had always wanted to drive a car since I was little tike. It stems back to when I was a small, and my grandfather got me a car seat equipped with a steering wheel and horn. This car seat slipped over the front seat to give me a clear road view. Our family always put safety first; no kids rolling around in the back seat for us. I couldn't wait to be 16 years, one month, and one day old. That was the law in Indiana when I was a teen.

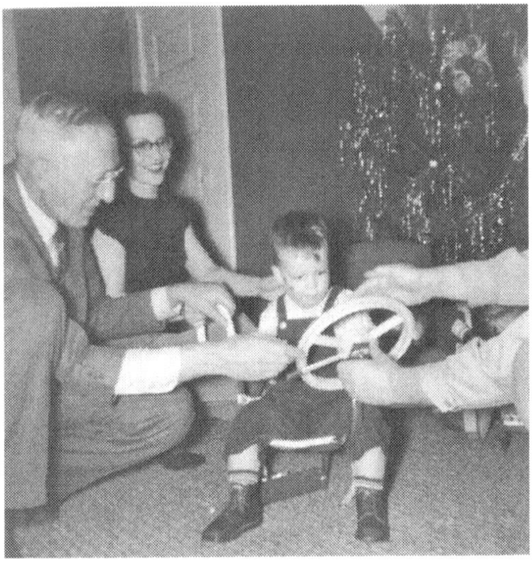

first car seat

You could get a beginner permit at 15, which I did the day I was legally allowed. The beginners' permit lets you drive with a parent in the car. My mother let me drive her car by myself in our driveway. In the winter, I would warm the car, turn it around, bring it up to the house, and scrape the frost off the windshield. That was pure heaven for me to do.

My mother would take me out to practice driving frequently. She found a panic button she installed on the passenger side dashboard that she could push when nervous. It wasn't hooked up to anything, but it made her feel more secure. I remember her pushing an imaginary brake pedal on the passenger side when I was going too fast. These practice sessions prepared me for the driver's training class I took during the summer at my high school. This class was to prepare us for the state driving examinations. Every day we would get classroom instruction geared around the state-required driver's manual and watch films about bloody car crashes to scare us about driving recklessly. We also would go out driving with an instructor and three kids to a car, practicing different scenarios. The instructor's car had a brake installed on the passenger side, which saved many lives over the years.

After taking driving lessons from my parents and getting the school driver's education certificate, I was ready to take the Indiana State required written and driving examination. You only got a few chances to pass the exam, so I was nervous, but I passed both on the first try. I was now fully qualified to get my license.

On the appointed day when I was sixteen years old, one month, and one day, I had my mother drive me to the license bureau before 8 AM so I could be the first in line to get my license. I gave the clerk my fee and paperwork showing I passed their test. Boom, I was officially licensed by 8:15. What a proud day.

I drove home very excited that I could now drive anywhere I wanted by myself. When we got home, my mom said, 'Dang, we should have stopped at the store. We need some milk.' Faster than a speeding bullet, I volunteered, "I'll go to the store," and grabbed the keys. Reluctantly my mother said, "OK, but be careful." I'm sure I reassured her I would indeed be careful.

It was 9 AM as I pulled into the grocery store parking lot, driving my parents' brand-new Olds 88; it was a long beast of a car. I had tuned the radio to the rock & roll station listening to some great '60s music. I spotted a parking spot close to the front door and pulled into that opening. I was too close to the car and pulled in too sharply, scraping the front door, back door, and rear quarter panel on the car's bumper next to me. I can still hear the sound of crumpling metal. My heart sank, and my stomach flopped as I exited the vehicle to see the damage. Our car had a long deep dent, and the car I had hit had no damage to its bumper. Forty-five minutes after receiving my license, I wrecked the family car. "Holy Crap, Batman!'

I went into the store, got the milk, drove home, and told my mom. She flipped out and yelled at me all day until my dad came home. I thought he would continue to yell at me, but he just said he wasn't turning that into insurance, and I would have to get a job to pay for the damage. I said but isn't that what insurance is for. He said 'Yes, but they will raise the rates. Start looking for a job.'

The next day I took the car to a body shop owned by a neighbor to get a friends and family discount. I remember Wimpy, the owner laughing as he gave me the estimate. He predicted I would become one of his best customers. He fixed the car and let me pay on time.

My high school counselor requested some boys to help unload rail cars after school. This company processes wood veneer for furniture manufacturers. They got big skids of wood veneer and further processed them into parts to be laminated onto furniture. So, I signed onto this crew after school whenever they got a new shipment and unloaded these crates. They couldn't use forklifts because this product was so delicate; we had to pick up the crates individually, move them to the freight car door, and then manually move them to the warehouse. Hard, dirty work that I got paid very little for. I would take all my money earned each week and pay off my body shop debt. You would think I learned my lesson on being a safe driver.

One of my favorite teenage activities in our small town was 'cruising.' Driving slowly around town in a loop so that you can see and be seen by others. It was an expression of freedom granted by possessing a driver's license. In my hometown, Friday night was a steady stream of cars slowly driving around town in a big loop, starting at the A&W root beer stand around the town square looping back to Mickey-T's supermarket parking lot, then back to the root beer stand. Usually, there were cars full of boys showing off their hotrods and cars full of girls all getting out of the house from under the supervision of the parental units.

Occasionally boys would initiate drag races at stop lights, drawing attention from the police officers. Still, it was mostly just kids loitering in parking lots chatting up the opposite sex. We would all chip in a couple of quarters to the driver for gas money; a dollar's worth of gas would last the evening.

It was my turn to drive my crew around one August night, so I got permission to take the family 'Olds 88' out for Friday night cruising. Yes, the car I had previously dented on my first day of driving. It was NOT the babe mobile like the tricked-out 57 Chevies all the cool guys had. I picked up my buddies Wilton, Darryl, and Sam. Darryl shouted, 'Shotgun!' so he took the prime seat.

It was a warm August evening, so everyone had their windows down with radios tuned to WIBC radio playing all the great Beach Boys and Jan & Dean cruising songs. It was an exciting innocent evening of fun till things turned dark. A car full of girls in front of us sped off, diverting from the regular route; Wilton shouted…" Let's Follow

Those Chicks." I floored it and caught up with them, heading down a residential street. They spotted us following them and immediately started evasive maneuvers turning on side streets, left and right, until we lost them. We decided to abandon the chase and head back to the regular route. As I was driving down this narrow side street, I saw a car approaching us with two girls sitting on the hood of a car leaning back on the windshield. The car was driving fast while the girls were trying to keep their skirts from flying up in the breeze and not sliding off the car. In my defense, it was easy to see how I became a distracted driver. It wasn't my fault.

It was a narrow street with cars parked on both sides, so I aimed my car toward the curb to give these young ladies more room. My head involuntarily twisted to get a better view of this marvel of feminine guile. As they flew past and my head swiveled, evidently, my hands (Ten and Two) on the steering wheel jerked right. Instantly, I drove over the curb and hit a fire hydrant. Fortunately, I was going slow, and it was just a glancing blow. Thankfully I didn't knock the hydrant off its mounting, spraying water everywhere. The only damage was to the front quarter panel of the car and my ego.

Everyone was silent as I drove them home; no one offered to chip in repair money as they did earlier for gas. How would I tell my parents I had wrecked their car again that I was still paying off the first wreck? When I got home, the house was dark, so I assumed my parents had already gone to bed. I quietly sat alone in the living room rehearsing my speech. I must have sat there for an hour when I finally got the courage to knock on their bedroom door and got no answer. It turns out they had gone out for the evening and had yet to return. I had to wait until morning to deliver the news. Wimpy laughed when I went to get another estimate, and he said somehow, he knew I would become one of his steady customers.

I'm pretty sure I still hold the world record for the fastest car wreck right after getting my driver's license.

The day I met Jesus

When I turned 16, my parents wanted to take a family car vacation to Mexico. Being a typical teenager, I didn't want to go on a family vacation. That time with two much younger siblings, plus my parents, just did not seem exciting. I argued that I could take care of myself at home just fine. Somehow, we reached a compromise. I would go, but only if I could bring a friend my age to avoid too much time with the little kids.

The family car was a large Oldsmobile 88, but it would still be a tight squeeze: two adults, two teenagers, two tweens, and luggage. The car had a large trunk, but more luggage space was needed. The solution was a rack added to the roof. I still don't understand, but somehow, I talked the parents into bringing my Honda Trail 90 motorcycle along. A rear bumper mount was added to hold the scooter, or "motorcycle," as I called it. The Honda was a great little scooter with two easily changeable rear gears that would convert from trail to street mode, allowing it to go 50 miles an hour on the road. I think the main reason it was brought along was to separate the teenagers from the rest of the crew when we became too rowdy. We could follow along

Honda 90 - Yellow Banana

behind the car and give people in the car a break. During the test loading of the car, it was quickly determined that better shock absorbers were desperately needed. With that modification accomplished, we set off on our trek from Indiana to Mexico and points between. Sadly, no photos survive of this car with luggage rack and scooter. I am sure many who saw us on the road remember this sight. It was a good thing gas was cheap back then. It couldn't have gotten good mileage with all the people and goods strapped on.

The car was loaded, and off we drove to Mexico. My buddy Bruce and I had just gotten our driver's licenses, so we got to drive on the U.S. freeways. This gave us plenty of practice time to practice our newly acquired driving skills and provide the parental units a break from driving. At that time, Mexican laws didn't recognize U.S. car insurance so we couldn't drive the car in Mexico. When we left Texas and went to Mexico, Chihuahua City was the first city we stopped in the early afternoon for the night. At that time, there were about 150,000 inhabitants. This would be a place to eat and sleep as it was not a tourist destination. The following day we would be heading to our ultimate goals of Guadalajara, Mexico City, and Mazatlán, where we had planned to begin our tourist activities.

Bruce and I had two years of high school Spanish under our belts and erroneously believed we could speak Spanish. Sitting in the Chihuahua hotel room, we were bored and told my parents we were going for a ride on Trail 90 'motorcycle.' The place we were staying at was a modest resort. We wrote down the name and address in case we got lost. We could use our Spanish skills to ask for directions. At sixteen, we had no fear since we figured we were invincible. Besides, what could go wrong, right? It was time for some adventure in a foreign land. We put on our helmets and went off on the Yellow Trail 90 scooter to cruise the streets as we did at the root beer stand in our Hoosier hometown.

We stayed on the main road into town to find our way back easily. We were having a great time seeing the sites. At a stop light, a young Mexican youth about our age pulled up next to us and motioned for us to pull over to the curb. He was smiling, and we pulled over despite a bit of trepidation. The guy was riding a loud, tricked-out chopper with ape hanger handlebars. He wore a black leather vest with a red bandana around his head. He looked like a young Danny Trejo from the movie 'Machete.'

We introduced ourselves in our limited Spanish, and he said his name was "Hay-SOOS." He was very interested in the Yellow Trail 90 bike, and we figured out he had never seen anything like it. His English was about as good as our Spanish. We told him we were from Indiana, and he responded by saying, "Indy 500". Our new friend said "Vamanos," which means "Let's go," so he roared off, and we "putted" along behind as best we could. At the next light, several motorcycles were stopped along the curb. Our new friend shouted, "Mira, los gringos en el plátano amarillo, Vamanos" Now we had a group riding together; what fun. (FYI, Mira, los gringos en el plátano Amarillo means Look at the gringos on the yellow banana, Lets Go).

The group started going on side streets and through back alleys. We had yet to learn where we were or were heading, but the group kept growing. By then, there were 20 bikers, led by our new friend. It was getting late, so we pulled over and told our buddy we needed to return to the resort but didn't know how. "No Problemo," to follow him.

Our entourage of bikers came roaring up to the resort entrance, and we thanked him for his help and said we enjoyed the Chihuahua tour. We asked them if they wanted to come in as our guests and "jugar cartas" (play cards). We went to the cabana in the courtyard and started playing cards. I asked our new friend how he spelled his name. He spelled it for me; J E S U S, "Hay-SOOS" I said, "Jesus?" he said, "No, it's Hay-SOOS." Being a very naïve 16 year old from a small Hoosier town, we had little exposure to Hispanic culture and didn't know this was a common naming practice. We were having lots of fun when the hotel manager came in and started yelling at the bikers, telling them they weren't allowed in the resort. I spoke up and said that I had invited them as my guests. He didn't care and continued to yell at my new friends. They left, and we returned to our rooms.

The manager came to our rooms and spoke to our parents. When the manager left, my parents were extremely upset with Bruce and myself. First, we were kicked out of the resort immediately and needed to repack the car and find another place to stay for the evening. Second, apparently, we had been running around with a bunch of Hell's Angel Bandido's. We could have been lying dead in some alley with our throats slit. I said, "But Mom, we had Jesus with us the whole time." Obviously, the novelty of the yellow banana scooter and two boys too dumb to be scared kept us from serious harm.

Most Embarrassing Christmas Gift

It was Christmas 1973 when I was newly married and gainfully employed. I was now an adult and had many people for whom I was expected to purchase gifts. I went to the mall armed with a list of items to locate and secure in a single manly power shopping spree. I saw a store temporarily diverting me from my mission as I entered the mall. The first store I saw was Fredericks of Hollywood, the precursor to Victoria's Secret. I walked by several window displays that caught my eye. I told myself I'd bet my wife would appreciate a Christmas present from this store.

So, I went in with no specific ideas; a sales clerk, seeing I was dazed, asked if she could help. I said something brilliant like, "Umm, sure, maybe." The clerk started asking me specifics about sizes and styles. I had no clue what she was talking about, so she steered me to a rack of one-size-fits-all garments.

I said garment, but there wasn't much to these items made from stretchy, flimsy, see-through fabric that wasn't designed for warmth. The designer had placed tiny bits of material in strategic locations. After assurances from the clerk that these were very popular and one size fits all, I told her I would take a red one. I was not comfortable in this store at all. After she rang up her easiest sale of the day, she asked if I wanted a gift box and bag. I nodded yes. She returned with this huge pink sack with the Fredericks of Hollywood logo. I sheepishly asked if they had a smaller bag; she said this was the only bag.

OK, one impulse item purchased with my entire list still to procure. I headed back into the mall concourse to the next store. As I was walking, I noticed people staring at me; I finally figured out it was the giant pink bag. One lady grabbed her young daughter's hand and moved quickly away from my path. The rest of my shopping list was purchased rapidly to avoid the stares.

So now was the next step: getting the presents wrapped. I was and still am the worst wrapper ever. I asked my new wife to wrap my gifts except hers. I figured I'd do those myself. It was very close to Christmas, and I still needed to finish that task. At my job, a high school girl working half days as an office intern announced she was wrapping presents to raise funds for one of her clubs at school. I went out to my car and retrieved the box from the trunk. I gave it to her with specific instructions: "Whatever you do, don't look inside the box." About 15 minutes later, she returned to my office with a bright red face and the wrapped present. I asked her if she had looked inside the box, and she just turned and walked out of the room. Yep, she looked. Now, the other ladies in the office were all snickering. She, indeed, had looked and told the rest of the office crew.

So far, this brilliant idea of mine was a colossal flop. It was now Christmas Eve, and it was time to go to my wife's grandparents for their traditional gathering to open one present at their house after dinner. My wife and I got home from work at the same time. She gathered presents for her folks and grandparents and one for each of us to open. Yikes! She grabbed 'The Present.' While she went to get her coat before we rushed out the door, I grabbed 'The Present' and swapped it with another one for her. Wow, that could have been a disaster. I went to the garage for a moment before we left. I didn't know she noticed I swapped her present, so she un-swapped it back to 'The Present.'

We were at the grandparents' house and had just finished

dessert, as was their tradition before we started opening the presents. All was going well; my mother-in-law had just opened my gift to her—a large box of those chocolate-covered cordial cherries, truly her Christmas favorite. For a very short moment, I was the good son-in-law. I looked over, and my wife had already taken the wrapping paper off 'The Present'; she was removing the tissue paper from the box, and my brain froze. I couldn't move fast enough to knock the package out of her hands. She was already lifting this flimsy piece of fabric and holding it high so everyone could see what a pervert I was. My father-in-law was fuming, my mother-in-law, who loved wintergreen lifesavers, swallowed one whole, my sister-in-law chortled, and the grandparents almost went into cardiac arrest. The look in my wife's eyes was burning a hole right through my soul. Generally, after the present opening, their tradition was to play Pinochle, the card game. I forgot who suggested it was too late to start that game, but it wasn't very comfortable.

The car ride back to our apartment was sure silent and icy. That old favorite Christmas song, 'Silent Night,' sure took on a different meaning. I kept trying to explain that it wasn't my fault. I had taken "The Present" off the pile to take. I had tried to avert disaster. Steam was coming out of her ears, for sure. I explained I could exchange it for the black one if she didn't like red.

I'm not entirely useless. I can be used as a Bad Example.

Waffles

I distinctly remember the day early in the school year of my 7th grade my mother fixed me a delicious hot breakfast. I was in the middle of my growth spurt and eating anything not nailed down. Despite my enormous appetite, you could call me spindly, skinny, lanky, and gangly. This feast of waffles, bacon, scrambled eggs, toast, and OJ was unusual. My mother and I had clashed in the mornings since grade school. She was definitely not a morning person, and I was a gung-ho, full-speed-ahead kid when my feet hit the floor in the mornings.

Even in grade school, I fixed my breakfast before school. Usually, cold cereal with milk or maybe toast with cinnamon sugar. This was our agreed-upon method of not having a scene every morning. It's not that my mother wasn't a great cook. She would fix fabulous meals for dinners (except for the occasional liver and onions, yuck!). However, facing me without at least two cups of coffee in the morning was not her thing. Still, something must have gotten into her that day, and she surprised me with a glorious feast on a school day, no less.

Nothing else about the start of this day would have indicated the troubles ahead for this awkward teenager. My first class of the day was gym class. Our teacher, Mr. Zimny, was a former NFL Chicago Cardinal and a huge man. He played tackle in the NFL for five years and even won a championship in 1947. He was also very loud; gym teachers are always loud, right? I remember the first

Coach Z

day of 7th grade when he told us about his gym class rules.

We were all seated in the bleachers and listening quietly. Well, most of us were attentive. One of my classmates, Charlie, was chatting away, distracting the entire class. Mr. Z. had already warned this kid twice; actually, yelling at him is a better description. His booming voice echoed through the whole gym. After the third interruption, Mr. Z. walked up to the row where Charlie was seated and grabbed him by the ears, dragging him down the steps across the gym floor to the stage. Charlie's feet barely touched the floor as he was dragged across the floor while he was shrieking in pain. I was shocked at the escalation of punishment allowed in middle school, even in those days. Mr. Z. said, "Maybe now, with your ears properly stretched, you can hear my rules." WOW, we all were now totally intimidated by this teacher. All my teachers previously had been sweet and kindly grandmotherly types. This guy was like the drill sergeant from the Full Metal Jacket movie.

So, back to the day of the waffle breakfast, Mr. Z. decided we would play flag football for P.E. class that day. We were having a great time, and my team decided to call a play where we ran the ball on the right side of the line. The QB said we needed blockers out in front of our runner.

Somehow, I got my skinny body out in front of this horde and promptly got overrun from behind by my own teammates. I wasn't very fast, in addition to being scrawny. Bam, I was flat on my face with my right arm awkwardly pinned beneath me and in intense pain. I had never experienced pain like that before or since. I slowly got up and went over to the sideline, holding my arm, trying not to cry. Nobody missed me in the game. Soon, it was time to return to the gym and get dressed for classes.

Somehow, I got dressed using my good arm and went off to math class. I was telling one of my buddies about my injury. Bruce gave me the "walk it off, rub some dirt on it" pep talk. I was in intense pain and didn't see the humor in that. The class was about to begin when Bruce suddenly grabbed my arm and shook it vigorously to prove I wasn't injured. The pain was so extreme that I almost passed out. The pain shot from a 7 to Spinal Tap 11. Without warning, a stream of expletives came out of my mouth that would have shocked the entire 7th fleet of the US Navy. The math teacher was a relatively new and inexperienced teacher whose face turned red, but she said nothing. She just ignored the "F" bombs flying around the classroom. My buddy was profusely apologizing, and I eventually stopped cursing. Class proceeded like nothing happened, and I toughed it out the entire period. Somehow, I made it through the rest of the day and rode my bicycle home with my injured arm dangling loosely at my side.

When I walked into the house, my mother saw I was carrying my arm funny, and it had an extra bend in the forearm like I had two elbows. I thought she was going to throw up. She quickly asked me what happened as she gathered her purse to take me to the hospital. It was a Wednesday, and she realized that was the day all the hospital doctors played golf, so we went to an open local clinic.

X-rays were taken, and the answer quickly came back that I had a closed fracture of both the ulna and the radius. That was why I had a bend in my forearm. They knocked me out so they could set the fracture. When I woke up, my arm had a nifty cast. They sent me home with some painkillers and said to stay home from school for a couple of days for the swelling to subside.

I returned to school with my cast arm in a sling and an excuse note for my absence. This was the first time I had to go to the principal's office, so I was very nervous. Principal Sexton asked how I broke it, and I told him about the flag football game incident in gym class. He looked through some notes in his inbox and said he didn't have any reports of injury in school that day. He was getting worked up and said he would have to investigate why he wasn't notified. He told me he had insurance reports to fill out whenever someone got injured on school property. I told him it was probably because I didn't tell anyone. His jaw almost hit the floor.

The principal asked why I wouldn't have told anyone about the injury. I hesitated, but finally, I told him I was afraid of Mr. Zimney, the gym teacher. He busted out laughing and finally told me a secret about Mr. Zimney. He said he was rough on the outside but a teddy bear on the inside. He told me not to report to gym class that day so he could explain the situation to the gym teacher.

The next day, I reported to gym class. Mr. Z apologized to me and said he was sorry I got injured. He told me that I would be in charge of attendance for gym class until my arm healed. All I had to do was turn in the absences and sit on the bleachers watching class. I was surprised when report cards came out, and I received an "A" for P.E. during that grading period. He truly was a softy on the inside.

The story's moral is don't eat a heavy breakfast before exercising. My mother and I joked about that for a long time. I asked her to only fix a fancy breakfast on weekends when I could be sure not to hurt myself at school.

Better Living Through Chemistry

The statute of limitations has expired so I can tell you all this story from my misguided youth. Yes, I have all my fingers. Kids, plcasc don't do this. I am pretty sure the FBI, DHS, ATF, and several other alphabet organizations will be visiting your homes if you do. This is to be used as an example of what not to do when you are a bored teenager.

A few neighborhood brothers, Chris, Eric, and I, decided we needed to make our fireworks one day. A few other neighborhood kids were involved, but they are now in the witness protection program and asked me not to mention them. A recipe on how to make black powder was obtained.

This was way before the internet, so it took a fair amount of research. Gunpowder, also known as black powder, consists of a mixture of sulfur (S), carbon (C), and potassium nitrate (saltpeter, KNO 3). Sulfur plus carbon (in the form of charcoal) acts as fuel, while the saltpeter is an oxidizer. I continued my interest in chemistry in high school and had a 40-year career selling high-performance plastics. Who knew?

I am trying to remember where we ultimately found this recipe. It could be from reading Popular Science magazines or one of my trips to the library to escape the brutal summer heat.

We sourced these materials to see if we could obtain them cheaply and easily. The charcoal we knew we could get from our parent's bar-b-que; we would have to pulverize it into a powder via a few hammer blows. We went to several drug stores and found gallon-sized jars of sulfur and saltpeter on the back shelves.

To keep our project secret, we decided it best to split our purchases between different drug stores, Chris would go to one store, Eric to another, and then I would alternate doing the purchasing. The pharmacists might have noticed a pattern if just one person kept buying the supplies, got curious, and stopped our plan before it started. I think prosecutors would call this willful intent a party's intention to knowingly and deliberately act or refrain from working in a particular manner or achieving a particular result. But let's not dwell on the legal side of this story. We were just kids having fun. Regardless, no adults seemed to care what we bought the stuff for.

I won't divulge the ratios of these ingredients, but we did several experiments to get optimal bang (no pun intended) for our buck. We immediately discovered that the charcoal needed to be very finely ground. Pounding it with a hammer left too many big clumps that didn't ignite evenly and caused too much smoke. Chris and Eric appropriated their parents' old-fashioned hand-crank coffee grinder to solve that. This machine produced fantastic charcoal powder. I have often wondered if their coffee tasted better having a charcoal aftertaste.

The other two ingredients were already powdery, making an excellent mixture. I will also say we took safety precautions. We knew using steel instruments around the final product could cause sparks and set off a catastrophe. Wooden spoons and aluminum pans were also appropriated from our moms' kitchens. We took our 3-part mixture and added water to dissolve the sulfur and sodium nitrate to form a single compound. We let this dry, hoping it would be like adding eggs to sugar, flour, and cocoa to make a delicious cake.

After we developed our best homemade black powder, we

set out toward our original goal - fireworks. We poured the powder onto the newspaper and rolled it up like burritos using a little tape. Our first products could have been better. When we lit the paper, it tended just to make a lot of smoke and flames. The next generation decided to wrap the "burrito" entirely with tape, except with one end we could light. These were fun as they would act like a jet engine with flames shooting out the end. We kept making different sizes of tubes until we found the best ratio of length and amount of powder to obtain liftoff. We were ready for our big test; this final prototype was placed in the middle of the street, set on fire, and stood back. It went scooting straight down the street at fantastic speed until it veered off the road into a neighbor's lawn, which burnt a large area of their well-manicured grass. Oops, this was the first intervention of parental units. We had to apologize and cool it for a while. The life of Free-Range 1960s kids wasn't always smooth.

While we were on shutdown, unable to shoot off our rockets, we were rethinking. Our re-focus was more on getting a Bang than rocket liftoff, more like firecrackers. We needed to devise a way to seal up all sides of our little paper tubes and still be able to light them somehow. Chris discovered that the local DePrez hardware store sold fuse. It came in coils; we could buy as many feet as we wanted. Yes, they would sell it to kids. They also sold dynamite, but we didn't think we could pull that off. Chris and I sent his younger brother, Eric, to buy ten feet of fuse for our testing. At first, we used a little to determine how fast it burned to determine when we needed to run away after lighting.

The first several trials of our firecrackers were duds, just lots of smoke. We then got the idea of using clay-rich soil in our backyards. We used a pipe to pound a deep hole in the ground; we filled the hole with our powder and stuck a length of fuse in the hole with enough above ground to make our getaway. We packed more clay into the top of the hole to make it sealed airtight.

Eric lit the fuse while Chris and I watched from a safe distance away as it successfully exploded. Yes, we blew a sizable hole in the ground with considerable noise. Our parental units finally decided that we had to stop this chemistry experiment. Someone’s mom might have even said, “You boys won’t be happy until someone loses an eye,” or some lame warning.

My “What did you do this summer” essay on the first day back at school could have been very exciting, but it also left me open to FBI scrutiny, so I wrote something boring about the family vacation trip. Kids today with helicopter parents must make do with TicToc videos. I feel bad for them.

High School Biology Experiment

I doubt you could do this today.

My father had a Guppy Grow operation as a hobby in the mid-1960s. When I say he had a grow operation, I mean his single tank of tropical fish in our living room exploded to over two hundred 20-gallon tanks in the basement of his office. This all started innocently with one large 50-gallon tank in our living room with many typical tropical fish like tetra, angel, swordtail, catfish, cichlids, and guppy like any average suburban family. You have seen the setup, colorful gravel for the bottom, fake plastic plants, filtration system, in-tank heater, fake rock cave, and lighted hood. The guppies were very prolific and started making babies almost immediately. This resulted in a second tank to hold the baby guppies so the other fish wouldn't eat them and BAM. He became a guppy breeder overnight, traveling the Midwest to Guppy conventions and selling wholesale fancy guppies to tropical fish dealers.

Male Guppy

The guppy (Poecilia Reticulata), also known as million fish and rainbow fish, is one of the world's most widely distributed tropical fish and one of the most popular freshwater aquarium fish species. The guppy is live bearing, reproducing every 25-30 days. Guppies originate from the northeast part of South America.

In the animal kingdom, females do most of the work, expending more metabolic energy on reproduction, so they are likely to be pickier about whom they mate with. That means the males must compete for the female's affection. Thus, males have no choice but to grow prettier feathers and do more elaborate courtship dances to compete with other males. This is also true of the guppy world; the female guppy is usually very plain-looking with little or no bright colors. Male guppies, smaller than females, have ornamental caudal and dorsal fins. Guppy breeders have developed various colors and patterns not found in the wild using selective breeding techniques.

Founded in 1965, the International Fancy Guppy Association's (commonly known as the IFGA) mission is to promote the enjoyment and the techniques of breeding fancy guppies to the IFGA's show standards. Yes, this group had competitions and conventions that were great family weekend events… NOT.

The basement of my father's work was taken over with racks and racks of 20-gallon tanks filled with guppies being bred for these competitions. It was a windowless pit with bad fluorescent lighting on a timer and heated to maintain a water temp of 80F set to mimic their natural environment in the tropics.

Picture a puppy mill without sad puppy faces and no Sarah McLachlan from SPCA singing sad songs, just the soft gurgling of the air bubbles of the tanks. The tanks had no colorful gravel, fake plastic plants, or mermaid figurines. The fish just did fish stuff; they ate, pooped, bred, and died.

This is where I came into the operation. My job after school was to wheel a large tank around to put a vacuum hose into each tank and suck up the fish doo-doo and a small amount of water that would be replaced with clean water treated to the proper PH and properly aged to eliminate the chlorine in city water. If any fish croaked, I would net them up and dispose of them. Yes, as you can imagine, that was a fun job. It sucked, literally. Did you know a guppy can't fetch a ball, roll over, or be a boy's best friend? Most parents give the birds and bees talk; I watched female guppy's bellies swell till they gave live birth of 20-120 fry at a time.

These fish mature very quickly and can start breeding at ten weeks with a quick 25–30-day gestation cycle, making it easy to use selective breeding techniques to enhance cosmetic features like color or tail size. My father would select a few male fish from each liter for future breeding; the rest of the litter would be sold to a guppy wholesaler that supplied tropical fish stores around the Midwest.

Biology Experiment

When I was in sophomore biology class, my teacher, Doc Barnett, had us do a biology experiment of our choosing. He had a very hands-on method of teaching. We dissected grasshoppers and labeled the body parts on charts. We also dissected live frogs, which reminds me of this poor girl whose frog wasn't properly pithed (a procedure used to immobilize a biological specimen), and the frog jumped into her lap with guts following. She shrieked out of the classroom and is probably still in therapy 60 years later. Doc was very open to any idea of experiments. He was one of our legendary teachers.

I pitched my project to him, and he enthusiastically said, "WOW, Go for it." I told him about my dad's guppy mill, the guppy eugenics project. One problem I saw with my father's breeding program was that he just used the male guppy esthetics to select for the next round of genetic modification. That was only half of the breeding equation. The female typically exhibited no visible signs of what her offspring would look like. If you bred a blue male to a yellow female, you might get green offspring, not the better color blue you were hoping for. The female guppy was bland grey-greenish with no distinguishing dorsal or caudal fins. My experiment was going to take the guesswork out of the equation.

If you aim to develop a bright red guppy, you don't want to use a female with blue genes. How can you tell what the female genetics are visually? I designed a project to add testosterone to the female guppy tank to enhance her genetic color genes visually. I hypothesized that testosterone was what made the male guppy exhibit their colors. Would adding testosterone to the water with the females show her genetic colors?

OK, I had the ready supply of guppies and the teacher's approval of my experiment. I went to the local pharmacy and told the pharmacist my plan. Easy Peasy, I left the drugstore with a bottle of testosterone and a rough plan of proper dosages per gallon of water. The pharmacist wanted me to let him know the results. WHAT? Who gives a bottle of testosterone to a teenage boy without a prescription? Today, the DEA would have the pharmacist locked up for years.

OK. I got eight female guppies from one liter so that they would all be sisters with the same genetic strain. I had four tanks for the trials. One tank was a control tank and received no testosterone. Tank 2 would get one drop per day, Tank 3 would get two drops, and Tank 4 would get four. Each tank got fed the same regular guppy food. I had two fish per tank in case one fish croaked for some odd reason, like jumping out of the tank at night to evade Dr.

Josef Mengele's crazy experiments.

I took notes each day about the health of the fish and any visible changes. Slowly, I started seeing results; I saw the females in Tanks 2, 3, and 4 beginning to have color development. The fish in Tank 4 had the most color, and Tank 1 still had zero color. I took a Polaroid photo to record my results. Each week, the fish took on more and more color. They were from a liter where the males had large red tails. After three weeks, Tank 2 was a light pink hue; Tank 3 was an intense salmon color; Tank 4 was a dull red, and Tank 1, the control group, was an intense green-grey color, their normal color in nature.

My experiment produced the predicted results but didn't change breeding selection. The fish didn't tolerate the human testosterone and began getting sick. Tank 4, who had the highest dose, showed signs of TMS (teenage male syndrome). They spent their entire time driving around their tanks in muscle cars, burning rubber at each stoplight. They succumbed first, with the other groups following shortly afterward.

Doc Barnett gave me an A for my scientific method procedure, which consisted of systematic observation, measurement, experimentation, hypothesis formulation, testing, and modification. I still am surprised at how easy it was to get a bottle of testosterone, but this was where I obtained jars of Sodium Nitrate in my early days making pipe bombs. Better Things for Better Living...Through Chemistry was a 1935 DuPont slogan that has proven problematic in hindsight.

April 22, 1967

Me at Age 16

This is an essential date in my history. It may be hard for you to believe, but back then, I was a skinny, geeky, gawky teenager. I was starting to become interested in this thing some of my friends were doing called "dating." After much consultation with my inner psyche, we both concluded that I desperately needed some "date bait" to convert this from the idea stage into a reality.

After briefly exploring several overly optimistic options: adding 50 lbs. of muscle onto my svelte 6'0", 130lb body, obtaining a cool muscle car, ditching the black horned rim glasses, finding some "cool" madras shirts, etc. I had another conversation with my inner psyche; we launched a new plan, and the optimism of the adolescent male is very driven. Never, never, never give up.

We (me, myself, and I) determined that a "special event" was needed to detract from my lack of muscles and no cool car to possibly attract some interest. I scrounged up some money and purchased tickets for an upcoming concert in Indianapolis. This new group was touring the country, "Simon & Garfunkel," a folk-rock duo consisting of singer-songwriter Paul Simon and singer Art Garfunkel. This would be my "date bait" to secure an evening with a girl.

Our plan was working perfectly; I now had two tickets to see Simon and Garfunkel at Clowes Hall at Butler University in Indianapolis. Also, permission was secured to use the family "Olds 88". Just one more little detail remained .... I needed a date.

Looking back at this part of the plan, I can now see how it foreshadowed my future career in Sales. I cross-referenced our HS yearbook and the local phone book to begin the telemarketing process. The pressure was on, and the concert day was getting near. I grabbed the family phone and stretched the cord into the bathroom, where I could close the door for privacy. I combed my hair to get psyched into the spirit of my mission.

So, I started making calls; I was amazed at how many girls said, "George, who?" One girl was still confused when I reminded her that we were lab partners in Biology. These minor setbacks didn't faze me since I was on a mission. I continued to make call after call. Finally, I got a different answer – This girl said, "I will have to ask my mother." That response confused me. Was that a Yes or another Dodge? What do I do now? It was getting late, so I stopped calling for the evening with plans to resume the following evening.

I was walking down the hall in school the next day when this girl stopped me and said, "My mother said it was OK; I can go." A girl spoke to me… my brain locked up, I froze, and I think I said something brilliant like "To what?" Then I remembered… ohh yes the concert. I had made my first date with a girl. Woohoo! I didn't realize it then, but I had just secured a date with my future wife. The story's moral is to have a plan and work the plan.

Junior High School Cafeteria

I don't remember much about the classrooms in Junior High, but I remember the cafeteria like it was yesterday. There is perfect logic in why junior high school separates primary from high school, at least for the males of the species. It is a holding pen like the cattle feedlot where calves are grown to complete development. This is a critical time when the male brain is characterized by many changes that profoundly impact our cognitive, emotional, and social lives. The hormonal and physical changes explode almost overnight at this age. Not much educational content can be installed during this time.

Experts say one of the most noticeable transformations of the adolescent male is the growth of the prefrontal cortex, the region responsible for decision-making, impulse control, and complex reasoning. I will tell you a few stories I remember from my journey through Junior High. Let me know if you think my prefrontal cortex was functioning normally.

The cafeteria in my junior high school might have foreshadowed George Lucas's Mos Eisley Cantina scene set in a tavern on the remote planet of Tatooine, populated by a wild assortment of aliens that Obi-Wan Kenobi called a "wretched hive of scum and villainy."

My Junior High school was built in the 1910s originally as the town's high school. As the population grew, they had to create a separate new High School, and this building became the Junior High. It was an enormous three-story building with the classrooms having 12ft ceilings, stone hallways, and stairs everywhere. The front entrance had massive twin staircases that had designated traffic flow. You know, Up the Down staircase or something like that.

The cafeteria was in the basement of the newer wing. We would rush out of class when the bell rang to get in line for the government-funded Type A hot lunch. If you lived nearby, you could go home for lunch, but I had to stay. I had grown almost a whole foot that year and was constantly starving, so it was imperative not to get in the back of the line. I practically leaped down the stairs, taking two and three at a time to gain early entry to the food line. It seemed like hours, but the line moved fast. The boys constantly yelled and arm-punched each other while a duty teacher arbitrated the "No Cuts" disputes and issues that arose daily.

The cashier was first inside the cafeteria, and you could pay daily or have a punch ticket. You then got your plastic tray and started going down the line to the various lunch ladies serving each item. I always got everything offered, even if I didn't want to eat it. Once inside the lunchroom, we sat at these picnic-style tables with benches. Then, the trades would begin; you would try to barter your unwanted food for a more desirable item. My nickname was Vulture. As I reached across the table for something on my buddy's plate, I would say …." You gonna eat that?" I frequently got stabbed with a fork, trying to steal their food. I still have a few scars visible where a fellow inmate maliciously forked me. Yes, ' Hey, you forked me' remarks would cause instant insane laughter among the boys.

I swear the prisoners in Papillon were given more food than we got. After bartering, stealing, and licking my tray clean, I would wait for the line to end. I would then take my tray back to the end of the line and beg the lunch ladies for leftovers. They weren't supposed to do that, but I always told them stories like kids in China were starving, so why throw away good food? They frequently took pity on me and scraped any remaining morsels onto my tray. I was so skinny my shadow wasn't seen until college.

One day, they were serving stewed prunes with our meal. My buddy Bruce announced he loved prunes. The rest of us said yuck but took them as we passed down the line. Once we sat down, the challenge began. We all started passing our prunes over to Bruce, who was thoroughly delighted. He ate all the prunes on our table and was still hungry. He had eaten ten prunes at this point. We started going to the other tables, asking for their prunes. Soon, Bruce had a massive pile of prunes on his plate. It was like the hardboiled egg scene in Cool Hand Luke. We started announcing the number after each prune he ate. I remember the teacher/guard chuckling out loud. Bruce finally announced he was done at twenty-two just as the bell rang to return to class. What a magnificent record that was.

Bruce and I were on the junior high track team, so after school that afternoon, we went to practice as usual. After those prunes fermented in his stomach all afternoon, he looked a little green. The coach had us running laps as a warm-up. Bruce was obviously in distress; he would jog very slowly and then burst into a sprint as fast as he could when we got near the outhouse on the far side of the quarter-mile oval. He would soon rejoin us on the track and repeat the same behavior several more times. The coach asked me, "What's up with Bruce?" I said, "I don't know; he was fine at lunch when he ate twenty-two prunes." The coach shook his head and laughed, 'You idiots, prunes are a natural laxative. He is probably in there pooping his prefrontal cortex out."

The cafeteria had a rotating list of about fifteen items—nothing extraordinary like the pizza that today's kids get. I liked most things; my favorite day was chili with peanut butter sandwiches. That was pretty tasty, and they always had extra for hungry boys. Standing in line, we could always smell what was on for that day. Tuna Casserole was the worst yuck we (my buddies) hated those days. I ate it, but it was in protest. We always made jokes about it. The cooks always spread potato chips on top before baking them, so they were sometimes slightly burnt on the edges. This led to a rumor that they weren't really potato chips; they were scabs from the leprosy ward at the hospital. This is so gross that I won't admit I started this rumor. Looking back, it must have been part of that decision-making, impulse control, and complex reasoning thing we lacked.

Every day, while we stood in line waiting to get into the food line, the same cliques of kids were usually together. My group was the nerds, dorks, and geeks crew. Some of us had started our growth spurts and voice changes. We were a motley crew with squeaky voices that led to much teasing and jostling while we stood in line impatiently waiting for our grub. One day, a girl named Ramona stood behind us. We were trying to act so cool because she was one of the girls in our class who had 'developed' over the summer.

Yes, we noticed these things—the Annette Funicello syndrome. I don't remember all the names we called them, but some were Buzzingas, Bazookas, Jugs, Melons, Hooters and Boobies. Remember, this was before we had developed our impulse control.

So, that day, we were being extra rowdy and punching each other's arms more than usual. This led to shoving, and I got pushed hard and stumbled backward. I swear my elbow accidentally touched Ramona's breast; it wasn't intentional. She gasped, and I shrieked, "I'm sorry, I'm sorry, he pushed me." Then, everyone in the line looked at Ramona. Her breast was now concave. She screamed! I thought I broke her boob. Acck. She ran off somewhere. We soon realized Ramona had not really developed over the summer but was merely stuffing her bra.

Amongst my buddies, I was now infamous. I skipped right past first base and made it to second base. Hitting a double, so to speak, on my first at-bat. Ramona never stood near us in line after that, and we never spoke of the incident. Despite knowing I had not really touched a boob, I didn't wash that elbow for a month. If this incident had happened today, I would probably have been suspended from school for unwanted sexual advances and be put in weekly classes to stop my sexual harassment behavior.

I often look back at my days in junior high, and most of them are just a blur. Just the cafeteria remains in focus. It's funny how food remains one of my favorite things.

Coach M

Our High School chemistry teacher was a very unique man. He was also my tennis coach, so I got to know him better than most teachers. I say he was our tennis coach, but we didn't think he actually knew how to play tennis. He was paid to transport us to tennis meets and supervise our after-school practice and meets. Coach M had been divorced and now had a second family, stretching his teacher's salary very thin, meaning he needed supplemental income.

My tennis career started my freshman year when our class was still in the junior high building. At that time it served grades 7-9 and the high school for 10-12. Later, a new addition to the high school allowed the freshman to join the rest of the high school. In the 9th grade, I learned through the grapevine that the entire high school tennis team was graduating. I never skipped school but was always interested in ways to minimize time spent in academic pursuits legally. It was common knowledge that the tennis team got out of school early on the days of their meets since tennis courts were not lighted, and they needed to finish before it got dark. When traveling to away meets, they got to leave school even earlier, sometimes around noon. This part-time approach to school piqued my interest. I didn't know how to play tennis, but I figured it was time to learn. Besides, girls dug athletes and tennis players are athletes. At least in my mind at the time.

I rounded up four buddies and explained my plan. We rounded up racquets and proceeded to learn the game. When the following school year began, and we arrived at high school, I asked who the tennis coach would be that year. The athletic director said he didn't think a team existed this year. I told him about the five ambitious sophomores ready to volley and serve for the 'Golden

Bears.' That's when Coach M got hired at the last minute. The tennis team played in both the spring and fall seasons.

In the fall season, we played teams in our athletic conference, and the spring focused on the geographical region. Our sophomore year was a learning and rebuilding experience. Yes, we got whooped most of the time. The coach was entertaining; our car rides to other schools were always filled with stories and jokes, and we left school early.

Coach M was very encouraging but didn't have many tennis skills to pass on. We were on our own to improve our skills. The Shelbyville Park system had many adults playing tennis during the summer. So, we pledged to play as much as possible over the summer. Our skills improved over the summer, and girls started hanging around the park, watching us hone our skills and build our muscles. My plan was working to perfection.

Next year was my junior year, and also the year I took chemistry. Coach M was the chemistry teacher, and to say he had a wildly unconventional teaching style was kind. Since he knew the guys on the tennis team, we were his targets for Socratic torments during class. We were always called on first to answer his impossible questions. His tests and grading were designed to make getting regular A, B, and C grades impossible. Most people were getting 15%, maybe 40% for top students, and zeros were common. We always felt like we were always failing but were learning tons. He would curve the grades for report cards. He emphasized organic chemistry, which later helped me in my 40-year career in high-performance plastics. At the time, I couldn't fully appreciate what he was teaching.

The chemistry storage room was full of odd chemicals he

occasionally used for experiments. He once showed us as a joke a bottle labeled Butyric acid that smelled like vomit. Somehow, this became a prank around the school when, mysteriously, a few drops made their way into waste cans of unpopular teachers' rooms. The smell would linger for days since nobody could find the source.

Coach M loved to play pranks. He would tell his students he was from an alternative planet. He made up stories about this planet. It was the same size as Earth and in the same orbit around the sun. You couldn't see it because it was always on the opposite side of the sun. We, the tennis players, knew he was joking and trying to get people's imaginations working. Lots of students thought he was mentally unbalanced. I personally think it was just his lack of sleep. Coach M worked at the hospital several nights a week as a lab technician to supplement his teacher's salary.

We practiced and played tennis in the city park about a mile from the high school. We would all run down to the park, where Coach M would drive down at some point during practice. Often, he would give us his key to get back into the school gym locker room when he had to leave for his night job at the hospital. Unsupervised teenage boys were dangerous. The school had just completed building a swimming pool in the new part of the gymnasium complex. It became a race to see which athletic team could 'skinny dip' first in the pool. The challenge was issued among the teams. The tennis team had the advantage since we had no adult supervision. Lookouts ensured no one was coming down the hall, and the tennis team christened the new pool appropriately. The other teams cried foul; there were no witnesses, and no evidence survived, but we won.

As I have said, Coach M was a great teacher, but his sleep deprivation sometimes got the best of his intentions of being an excellent teacher. On the days he was exhausted, he would often show us films he had in the storage room. One movie we saw numerous times was "So You Want to Be a Pharmacist." One warm spring day, we came into class, the window shades were pulled down, and the lights were off. Coach M said he was showing us a film today.

Yes, it was the pharmacist film for the umpteenth time. I had chemistry class during lunch; our school didn't have room for everyone in the lunchroom simultaneously, so classes had assigned lunch times. Our designated time was at the end of the period. About 5 minutes into the film, Coach was snoring in the back of the room. It was hot, and we all wanted to leave since we had seen this film many times before. As I said, I never was a troublemaker in school, but I wasn't the most academic either. However, on this day, it was time to make a breakout. I quietly slipped to the back of the room and turned the projector off, and we then all tiptoed out of the room, gently shutting the door and leaving Coach with his dreams. We got an extra-long lunch period that day. Coach got some Zs, and no one was wiser. At least, that's what we thought.

We came back to find Coach M furious. The school board and principal were making the rounds of classes that day. They popped into Chemistry and saw no students, with the teacher sound asleep. Later, I fessed up to Coach, figuring he loved good pranks. Ha ha, I ran extra laps around the park for weeks after that little 'prank.' Surprisingly, Coach M's teaching contract was not renewed the following year.

"Did I do that?"

Victory Garden

I was a newlywed living the incredible life of DINKs (Dual Income, No Kids) when our landlord announced a second rent increase in two years. We decided to buy a house and start building equity instead of paying rent to some landlord. We had money in the bank; remember I said we were DINKs. We began calling realtors and scheduling visits to homes for sale. I arranged a visit with the president of our small-town bank, where my family had banked forever. I asked him how to get a loan to buy a house, how much down payment we needed, how many years would be the payments, etc. He laughed at me and said we were too young and should come back in a couple of years.

I walked across the street to their competitor; the president of this bank was the father of a High School classmate of ours. I asked him the same questions, and he responded much differently, "What house are you considering, and how much is the price?" Long story short, he said your grandfather knew my grandfather; I will drive by that house on my way home and do a drive-by appraisal. He called me the next day, said he would approve a 5% down loan for us, and told me how much the monthly payments would be. It was just a hundred dollars a month more than our current rent, and we would be building equity. Talk about your white privilege; we made an offer on the house the following week that was accepted. At the house closing, we signed the loan without filling out any applications or forms ahead of time. Easy Peasy.

So, what does this have to do with a garden? Fast forward a few months when the realization of being a homeowner sank into my adolescent brain. Though the twenty-two-year-old male brain may be done growing in size, it only finishes developing and maturing in the mid-to-late 20s.

The prefrontal cortex, the front part of the brain, is one of the last brain regions to mature. This area is responsible for planning, prioritizing, and controlling impulses. It was sinking in that many things like homeowner insurance, unexpected repair bills, and costly wife redecorating expenses were pushing household costs out of control. We needed to trim our expenses somewhere. The beer refrigerator for the garage however was missing from the list of expenses to cut.

As a newly suburbanized homeowner, I had begun watching PBS TV shows like Crocket's Victory Garden. This show made it very clear. I could reduce our food costs plus have better, fresh, healthier food. Remember the part about the adolescent male brain development… I had never done any gardening in my life.

I had a plan and knew just the person to help me execute it. I needed to talk to Fred, my wife's grandfather, a retired farmer and tinker extraordinaire. He saved my bacon when we first moved into our house. I had yet to think ahead about lawn care as a new homeowner. Lawnmowers were expensive, and our bank balance was low after closing our home. The yard was overgrown two weeks after we moved into our new house with one acre of grass. Our new next-door neighbor, who mowed his yard twice weekly, alternating directions, and bagged the clippings, was probably ready to call the HOA. I went out to see Fred. As a retirement gig, he repaired lawnmowers. There wasn't a small engine he couldn't rebuild. His garage was full of carbs, gaskets, and plugs for every Briggs and Stratton engine ever made. It just so happened that he had a couple of used mowers for sale. Five bucks, and I had myself a mower.

Fred always had an immaculate garden; I knew he could

help me get started in gardening. I went to their house and told him my plan to start a garden and that I needed instructions. Fred always smoked a pipe; as I was telling him about my goal, I saw him gripping his pipe tighter in his jaws and puffing away on his sweet cherry tobacco to squelch a guffaw. He knew my abilities.

He asked silly questions like where I planned to locate it and how big it would be. He gently told me my plan was doomed. "That location in your yard is too wet, and you won't be able to maintain that much as a new gardener." He suggested another part of my yard with more sun and better drainage. He also got me to think smaller. He told me I would need to strip the sod off and then add sand to the dirt because it had too much clay content. It was late in the growing season when I got my idea, so he said I had plenty of time to prepare for next spring. He said he would get a load of sand for me after I had it stripped of grass.

I am glad he convinced me to scale down my garden size; that sod removal crap was hard, challenging work. I cleaned it and called him, telling him I was ready. He showed up with sand in his truck and a small rototiller that he sold me for five bucks. We unloaded the sand, and he showed me how to use the tiller to work it into the soil. He said I needed to enrich the organic material in the dirt. I stared at him, and he said, "Put your grass clippings in here." As he was leaving, he said, make a list of what you want to grow, and let's talk next spring. I am sure he thought I would not follow through.

I dutifully worked the sand and grass clippings into the plot with my new rototiller. The soil was duly prepared. I watched every episode of Victory Garden that winter and marveled at his lovely results. My list was ready to discuss with Fred. Green beans, Bell peppers, Tomatoes,

Cucumbers, Corn, Squash, Lettuce, Spinach, Radishes and Carrots. Fred convinced me I didn't have room for corn, and I needed to drop two other items to make it more manageable. I told him about watching Crocket and was ready to get my hands dirty. He wished me luck as he drove off.

Our local hardware store always had an extensive selection of plants and seeds. Armed with my list of what I needed; I made my purchases. I was overwhelmed by the number of vegetable varieties, but I acted like I knew what I was doing and made my purchases. I even picked out a couple of different types of tomato starts. As I was heading to the counter to pay, I spied a little tag on a cute little plant, a small root with a few leaves. The label said Horseradish - a pungent root vegetable commonly used to impart a zesty, hot flavor to foods. Horseradish is a hardy perennial and can be grown in cold climates, full sun, or light shade. I didn't know what perennial meant, but I liked horseradish sauce on my steaks. This was going to be fun. I bought two.

Okay, long story short. The garden was a bust. The weeds did thrive in the newly tilled, aerated, fertilized soil. I realize now that I should have planted just a few seeds at a time rather than a whole row of radishes. Getting a bumper crop of 100 radishes ripe simultaneously doesn't make sense when your lettuce and spinach haven't sprouted yet. Who knew those cute little cucumbers could grow into baseball bat-size monsters overnight? I don't even know why I planted squash; I don't eat them. The carrots were all misshapen and ugly.

The tomatoes did grow very well, providing plenty of huge green tomatoes for tasty snacks for some critters. Just as I would notice a green tomato turning color, huge chunks would be stolen from my almost award-winning fruit the following day. I accidentally grabbed one of those large green tomato hornworm caterpillars with white V-shaped markings and prominent horns on his posterior. That took the joy of picking fresh produce right off my back porch. Yuck. I would like to know if I set a distance record when I flung it across the yard. The neighbors reported hearing a young girl screaming like a bear was attacking her. Add a pair of gloves to the growing list of expenses of this cost-saving life experience.

I did get a few nice green peppers, but the plants didn't tolerate the heat well and shriveled up. So far, the only item doing well was the pair of horseradish crowns I had purchased. Big leaves were taking over that corner of the garden. I decided I'd make this my crowning jewel of the garden. A little extra fertilizer certainly was needed. Long after the rest of the garden was dead, I was still watering my massive horseradish plants. This would undoubtedly be the biggest, best crop of horseradish ever.

I read that you harvest horseradish after the first frost. So, October arrived along with our first frost. I didn't have any frost on my pumpkins. I must add that to the list for the next planting season, but I did on my horseradish. The leaves had wilted. It was time.

I got my trusty spade out and began digging and digging. The clay was heavy and thick despite all the rototilling and soil augmentation I had done previously. It was tough digging, plus wet and cold, but I was determined to get the award-winning root out of the ground intact. I might have to use the wide-angle lens to photograph this beauty. It was getting dark, and the bottom of these roots was not in sight. I was tired, so I cut the root and called it good. I tossed the dirt into the hole and put the root in the garage to be processed the next day.

That following day, I looked at my bounty of horseradish root and decided I needed to go by at least a dozen mason jars to can this harvest. I cleaned the dirt off by scrubbing in the kitchen sink. It was time to start processing. I grabbed our handy stainless steel manual kitchen grater and started grating the root, producing little shreds of horseradish plus what I know now was a mustard-like oil compound called allyl isothiocyanate. It went very slowly, plus I began to choke and tear up. I put this project into high gear and got our handy electric blender. That beast of a machine made lots of frozen margaritas in an instant; it indeed could tackle a little horseradish. That is about the time Cathy returned home from Saturday morning shopping. I think I heard her saying over our coughing and choking – 'Get that shit out of my kitchen - NOW.'

So, after I opened all the windows, I located our extension cord to relocate my processing to the patio. I worked grating enough root for a couple of hours to fill the dozen jars I had bought. I added vinegar to preserve the grated root and sealed the jars. I put them in my beer refrigerator. I brought the blender back into the house. This immediately brought many complaints of odoriferous emanations. I washed and scrubbed that machine multiple times before we declared it unfit for future margaritas and tossed it in the garbage can.

My eyes were red almost swollen shut, but I was proud. I don't know anyone who ever canned that much horseradish during their first year of gardening. I also learned later that you must process it in a well-ventilated area and wear masks with proper eye protection.

I learned a few other things. The only thing harder to give away than baseball bat-sized cucumbers is quarts of horseradish. Evidently, the neighbors were all watching as I sat on my patio, grinding and choking.

I also learned what the word perennial meant. The following spring, after reviewing my analysis of gardening as a cost-saving idea, was something that I should NOT pursue again. I noticed the roots that I failed to fully extract from the garden had re-sprouted and thrived over the winter. I decided to obliterate this menace from my yard. I got out my $5 rototiller and chopped those pesky plants out of existence or so I thought. It wasn't long before I noticed that two plants were now over a dozen. I had created a bigger mess by producing many more plants. I decided to mow over them every time I cut the grass. I cried every time I mowed the yard until we moved several years later. I often wondered what the new owner of that house thought about me.

Moral of the story. Kroger has excellent prices on vegetables.

Icehouse

When I was fifteen, my parents co-signed a loan for me to buy an Icehouse. "Young man," they said, "it's time you learned the responsibilities in life." Like all the other industrious young men of that era, I guess they thought a paper route would not be enough of a challenge.

My icehouse was a self-contained ice cube-making machine that dispensed bags of ice for 50 cents. It was a small building, approximately 10ft by 40ft, consisting of two rooms, one for ice making and bagging and the other a freezer section for storing and dispensing ice bags. This building was located in a busy gas station parking lot who I paid a royalty for every bag of ice sold.

Icehouse

This project taught me many things about life and generated some money for my college fund. It also gave me lots of engaging life experiences along the way. It also was when I got my first checking account to make payments toward the loan, plus paying MRO (Maintenance, Repairs, and Operational) expenses on the equipment. See, I learned some valuable business vocabulary at an early age.

This machine was amazing. The icemaking room was very

compact, just big enough for one person to stand in front of the icemaker/ice cube bin and operate the bagger. Located on top of the ice cube storage bin were 16 racks of ice makers that automatically filled with water, froze the cubes, and automatically dropped them into the well-insulated bin below. The storage bin had a tiny conveyor operated by a foot pedal to fill the bags which then got stapled shut. I chose to use double-wall waxed paper bags over cheaper plastic bags. I felt the paper bags gave the customer better insulation properties, so the ice cubes were not frozen together in a large block. My customers didn't have to slam the bag on the ground to loosen the cubes. At least that's what the bag salesman said. Ha Ha. That was a joke and another life lesson. Don't always listen to salespeople. He just wanted to upsell me on the more expensive bags. I also had a water filtration system that made the cubes clear, not frosty. I am sure that the chemical I added was safe for human consumption.

When the bin filled up, the icemakers would automatically shut off. I could bag a bin full of ice in about 45 minutes, and it would take about 8 hours to fill up. I needed to show up three times a day to keep maximum production. This was needed during the peak summer months to stay ahead of demand. While I did my work, I kept a small AM radio there to listen to the best rock & roll station WIBC 1070 (which left the airwaves in 2021). I was able to listen to the latest greatest rock and roll songs of the Beach Boys, Jan & Dean and Beatles.

Like I said it was a tight space. I would fill about ten bags and then transfer them to the freezer room. One side of this room was where I had just bags of ice stacked up; the other side of the room was the ice dispensing racks. It was some angle iron, a screw conveyor, and a small electric motor. When customers put their money in the vending machine, a motor pushed the whole row of ice bags toward a dispensing chute. When a bag dropped off the rack, it dropped down the dispensing chute, triggering the motor to stop pushing.

Soon I learned to be very efficient at my duties. When I first arrived, I would go into the freezer and fill the dispensing racks with bags from the storage side. I would check the coin mechanism; it would need periodic maintenance when dirt from the coins would build up. I had some spray cleaner lubricant that would help it from jamming up. I would then bag any ice in the storage bin. I rode my bicycle two miles from my house several times daily. My goal was never to let the icemakers stop making ice. I was then free to do whatever I wanted the rest of the day.

At that point in my life, tennis was my passion, so I usually would head to the tennis courts to find a pickup game of tennis. The icehouse also left me enough time to get a second job. I joined with three other boys, and we rented ourselves out to be a roving hay baler team. Farmers would schedule us to come to their farms on days to be the muscle on the wagons to stack the hay bales and put them away in the barns. In addition to a free lunch, we would get a penny per bale. Usually, we would get about $10 each for the day's work. On the days of hay baling, I still needed to visit the ice machine three times. I paid myself a penny a bag for spending money and put the revenue balance toward my loan. I don't think anyone could say I was a lazy teenager. I certainly learned the value of hard work.

I discovered that even during peak sales periods, I could make more ice than I sold from the machine. So, when I was contacted by a man with several ice chests around town at various grocery and convenience stores, I considered branching into the wholesale ice cube distribution business. Multi-tier marketing way before Amway thought of it. I initially thought of him as a competitor. He didn't make his own ice, purchasing instead from a vendor in Indianapolis. After we talked, I realized I could make money selling him my excess capacity. We decided I would bag ice for him in his plastic bags and sell it as needed. I devoted a corner of my freezer to his stock. It was a bonus that his cute daughter, who happened to be my age, would often come along to help him pick up the ice.

Another lesson I learned was to be prepared for unexpected mechanical breakdowns. This complex machine with plumbing, HVAC, and electrical systems occasionally had issues. I remember vividly one day I arrived to find water leaking from the front door of the bagging room. The building was elevated on blocks, so the bottom of the entrance was several feet off the street level. I unlocked the door, not knowing that a pipe had burst, filling the bagging room with water. When I opened the door, a wall of water gushed out, knocking me off my feet and pushing me across the gas station driveway. Seeing a skinny kid get hit by a small tsunami gave the guys working at the station a great laugh. After I picked myself up and the shock wore off, I was able to find the main water valve and get it shut off. Thankfully the door to the freezer unit was watertight, and the stock was not ruined. I called the plumber, who came and made the necessary repairs. Other breakdowns occurred but none quite as dramatic.

I often walked into the freezer unit and found a space on the dispensing rack. The normal operating cycle would have a bag ready for the next customer at the end. I concluded this to be a design flaw, but then discovered it was possible to reach from outside into the chute up to where the ice bags dropped off the storage racks and pull one off for "free." I confirmed my theory one day. As I walked into the freezer unit, I heard some voices outside, a group of young men laughing, and I saw an arm come up the chute and try to grab a bag of ice. I decided to have some fun with this "petty thief." I grabbed his long-sleeved shirt and started pulling as hard as I could. He started screaming bloody murder, "I'm caught in the machinery, Help! Help!" I had a death grip on his shirt; his buddies were pulling on him, trying to free his arm caught in the "machinery." His buddies finally took his shirt off his back and let the "machine" keep it. I remember them cussing as I heard their tires squeal, leaving the scene of trying to steal a 50-cent bag of ice while almost losing an arm. Somewhere today, an old guy tells his grandchildren the story from 50+ years ago when he almost lost his arm in an ice machine. I kept that shirt as a souvenir for a long time.

I didn't know that this simple icemaking enterprise would turn me into part of a bootlegging operation. At that time, the sale of alcohol on Sundays was illegal in Indiana. My father was friends with the beer distributor in town; I learned that occasionally, on Saturday, a keg of beer would be dropped off at the icehouse to be held for pickup later. The operative word 'later' meant Sunday. People would call me to arrange a time I could be at the icehouse for their 'pickup.' The bagging room was always a cool 50 degrees, so it was the perfect temp for the keg. The beer customers would always buy several bags of ice for their kegs. I was glad to provide the service. The occasional one keg then turned into 2 or 3, depending on the weekend. There was barely room for me in that cramped space. It finally became too much, and I didn't even know I was breaking the law. So regrettably, I put a stop to this.

The summer months were the busiest for Ice Sales. During

the school months, I still went down multiple times a week to check on things, but the three times a day to bag ice dropped off sharply to a few times a week. There were spikes in demand during the holidays when people would need ice for parties. The nice thing about this job is that I could set my hours. Overall, the Icehouse experience was a great character-building experience. It taught me many things about life, people, and business. I sold my interest after a few years and cleared enough money to finance a couple of years of college at Indiana University. So, like Robert Matthew Van Winkle once said, "Ice Ice Baby"

Christmas Karnak

LIKE ALL KIDS, when I was a wee tike, I was amazed at the magic of Santa. Every Christmas, I would wake up to a mountain of presents delivered while I dreamt of visions of sugar plums dancing in my head.

What the hell is a sugar plum? I learned at an early age that a sugarplum is just a piece of hard candy made of hardened sugar in a small round or oval shape. It has nothing to do with fruit or dancing. I soon also heard from the big kids on St. Mary Street that Santa was my parents deceiving me into believing a scam. Santa Claus is a legendary character originating in Western Christian culture who is said to bring gifts on Christmas Eve of toys and candy to well-behaved children, and either coal or nothing too naughty children.

Who thought Santa could make it to every house in our little town of Shelbyville in one night? What other lies were my parents trying to feed me? Ha. I thought I would show my parents how well-behaved I was. I will play along with their deceit and pretend to be flabbergasted upon opening presents on Christmas morning. I vowed a mission to secretly learn what I would receive and keep my knowledge ahead of time.

When I was a kid, the parental units would hand me the Sears Roebuck catalog so I could window shop the toy pages for what I wanted from Santa. After circling almost every toy in the book, my mother told me to list just five things Santa might bring. Evidently, Santa needed more room in his sleigh. I pared down my wish list and took off the 101 chemical chemistries set, the official Red Ryder Carbine action, 200 shot, range model air rifle with a compass in the stock, and the pony, knowing my mom would veto Santa those items. At a tender age, I knew I needed to be reasonable and realistic. I kept my chemistry dreams on the back burner until I could obtain the goods on my own.

So, my wish list of 5 items was submitted to Santa. Fast forward to Christmas morning, I would sit in front of the tree, waiting for everyone to assemble. We always took turns opening gifts so everyone could see what everyone else had received. This is where I would perform my Karnak the Magnificent trick. I would pick up one of my presents and pretend to weigh it, remarking light vs. heavy. Then I would shake it and listen very intently to the sound, if any, before I announced what my gift was before I unwrapped it. I had fantastic accuracy guessing correctly, 8 out of 10. I never did 10 out of 10 because people would get suspicious.

Like all good magicians, I had secret techniques to get those results.

First, I used pre-Christmas recon skills that I honed each successive year. I would be very observant and make mental notes of where and when my mother went shopping during the holiday season. If it was to the five and dime versus a large department store in Indianapolis, I knew what kind of items she was buying, clothes vs. toys.

Second, I would hunt the house for Mom's secret hiding spots before she wrapped the presents. I acted quickly since she would wrap the presents shortly after purchase. It is easier to guess what gift you get if you see it before it gets wrapped. The hardest part is keeping the secret afterward. I would sneak around the house in stealth mode, looking under their bed, on closet shelves, in the laundry room, under dirty clothes in the hamper, or at the back of the garage. Mom was very sneaky. I had to be very subtle so that she didn't know I was on the prowl. I discovered they had been hiding presents at my grandparents' house one year. Those were the easiest to find since I was over there many weekends.

Thirdly, once the presents got wrapped and put under the tree, I would do the pre-Christmas guessing game with my mom. If a present got wrapped without me spotting it, I would pick it up and start the guessing game to watch my mother's reactions. After picking up the wrapped present, I would start making wild guesses to watch her face. I could tell when she got concerned that my guess was getting close to the truth. I would keep this up until she would yell at me not to wear out the wrapping paper.

Fourthly, if I had not been able to identify the present previously, I'd have to use my ultimate 'last resort' technique. My mother was an excellent present wrapper; she would let me watch her wrap if it wasn't for me. I learned a lot. My 'last resort' technique was to unwrap secretly partially the present so I could peak at the present or open the box with a crack. I would sneak down at night and use a single edge razor blade to slit the scotch tape very carefully in a few strategic spots so I could partially slide the present out to where I could see what it was. Then carefully slide the present back in and fold the paper exactly how it had been. The secret then was to get a piece of scotch tape slightly bigger than she had used and put it over her tape, thus hiding my deceit. Never try to take the tape off; it shows up. PS Don't cut yourself with the razor blade; that shows up and is hard to explain.

I would have gained almost complete knowledge of my presents by Christmas morning. I started with the concept that Santa wouldn't stray too far from my list, and I found many of them before they got wrapped or secretly unwrapped. On Christmas morning, I would shake my present and announce my guess. “This is a shirt, no wait; it is a sweater; I don’t hear the wrapping paper. It sounds much softer and bulkier than a shirt. I think it is a green sweater. Yes, a green sweater will match the brown pants in this other package”. Every year, my mom would get so surprised and angry that I always seemed to be able to have X-ray vision in my presents.

Maybe I Wasn't the Favorite Child?

As my family's first-born child, I had always assumed that my parents liked me best. As I reflect, maybe that assessment wasn't correct. At the time of these two stories, I was more than self-confident in my place in the hierarchy as the #1 child for many reasons.

The first Incident occurred on a family car vacation when I was eight or nine. We took frequent car vacations back then. The old red Mercury station wagon was outfitted with a custom-made mattress for the back portion of the wagon, with the third row of seats folded down for us kids to sleep. Automobile safety back then was not a thing.

Water Jug

I was assigned a task during this vacation. My job was to keep our gallon thermos jug filled with water. Thus, I was the designated "Gunga Din" of the Young vacation. It was a sweaty aluminum jug with a handle and spigot to dispense the water. The lid was screwed on and could double to be used to drink from and held an additional drinking saucer. Whenever we stopped at a motel, my instruction was to fill it with ice from the ice machine at the motel in the morning before departing. It would melt during the day, giving us ice-cold water without stopping somewhere for a hydration break. As everyone knows, vacations are about keeping schedules and beating the best times. At least that's what my parents said. Whenever we stopped, my job was to jump out of the car and find an ice chest, if available, or a cool water source. When we stopped at restaurants, the waitresses usually honored my humble request for ice. I distinctly remember one of them saying "You're a better man than I am, Gunga Din". Sometimes there was laughter as I ran back to the car, mission accomplished.

We often drove at night to escape the heat of the day because cars back then didn't have air conditioning. I was dozing in the backseat, and my siblings were back in the car's rear, sleeping on the mattress. I woke up when we pulled up to the gas pumps at a filling station. Without saying a word, I grabbed the jug and jumped out of the car to do my duty for the ice or water. The gas attendants told me the water hose was on the other side of the station and I was free to use it. I knew that to get the coldest, sweetest water possible, you had to let the water run for a while. Finally, completing my task, I returned to the pumps to climb back into the 'Old Merc.'

Only our car wasn't there. Oh my God! It was GONE. I mean, GONE! I looked around and couldn't see it anywhere.

I asked the attendants if my parents were coming right back. They looked mystified at me and then at each other. Here I was in the middle of who knows where in some far-off state in the middle of the night, alone with my water jug, sitting on the gas pump curb with two guys I might describe as

Goober and Gomer. As our family owned gas stations in my hometown, I was no stranger to gas stations. I wasn't too scared; I knew they were probably friendly people. It was getting late, and it seemed like forever. Goober and Gomer began flipping coins to see who had to take me home when they closed. I didn't cry but I was definitely scared.

It might have been 15 minutes, but to a young kid trying to be brave, it seemed like hours when I finally saw the old red Merc hurriedly pulling back into the station. My mother jumped out, all panic-stricken and apologizing to both me and the attendants for leaving without me. There were lots of hugs and kisses for me, not the attendants. My parents claimed they thought I was in the back asleep and hadn't done a head count. I explained I was doing the job that had been assigned to keep the water jug full. I notified the parental units when I exited the vehicle for the rest of the trip. I still had a nagging thought about whether they really considered not coming back for me.

The second incident occurred years later, during my junior year in college. I was coming home for a break between semesters, or maybe it was Christmas. I had my car at this point, so when I pulled into our house's driveway, a different vehicle was parked in the carport. I guessed maybe someone was visiting or the family car was in the shop being worked on. The time period was the early 1970s, and you might say my physical description was "long-haired, bearded, dirty hippie." I was carrying a large orange parachute bag full of dirty clothes. This was because my mother always enjoyed washing my clothes; I was making her happy.

I opened the unlocked door and shouted, "I'm home!" as I stepped inside the house I had lived in during my teenage years. As I plopped the laundry bag on the family room floor, I immediately noticed all the furniture, lamps, drapes, etc., were different than when I left a few months earlier. Just as I realized something was wrong, a lady I had never seen before came around the corner, panicked and shrieking at me, "Get the F*** out of my house." I don't remember everything she was yelling at me, but I certainly understood that my appearance, coupled with the recent Charles Manson murders, must have been extremely alarming.

I immediately backed up while explaining that I had lived there and was coming home from college. After several exciting minutes, this lady finally stopped yelling long enough that I could fully explain my bewilderment. She said they purchased the house and moved out a few weeks prior. She was finally convinced I meant no harm after I told my parents' names.

My next question was asking if she knew where my parents had moved. At this point, she nervously chuckled, "Your parents didn't tell you where they were moving?" She didn't have the exact address but knew the name of the housing division. It was a very small town, so I drove to that subdivision and drove around till I saw our family cars in the driveway. This time, I rang the doorbell and waited until my mother answered. My first words were, "So, you thought you could move without telling me where you were going?" Then I handed the large orange bag of dirty clothes to my mother. I told the story of the poor lady's shock. We all had a good laugh but in the back of my mind, I still to this day wonder if I ever was their favorite child. My wife (then girlfriend) swears my parents told me about their pending move, and I didn't listen like usual. Personally, I think it was the trauma of being left at the gas station all those years before. I could never entirely be sure where I stood after that.

Beer Keg at Home

During my first year of college, I warmheartedly recall the day my father had the ingenious idea to set up a beer keg at home. He acquired an old refrigerator, which he placed in the garage with the sole purpose of dispensing beer. Clearing out all the shelves, he created ample space for a half-barrel pony keg and a CO2 tank. A hole was drilled in the door to accommodate a single tap handle, allowing for the seamless pouring of a refreshing cold draft beer without having to swing the door open.

Garage Beer Fridge

This innovative setup meant he could savor the delights of draft beer without the hassle of heading to a bar. Being a self-proclaimed beer connoisseur, he often stressed the marked disparity in flavor between draft versus bottled or canned beer. His passion for freshness and taste was evident. He explained that draft beer maintains its freshness better than bottled beer as it is usually consumed closer to the brewery and is not as exposed to oxygen as bottled beer. The detrimental trio of oxygen, light, and heat degrades the quality of beer, causing it to lose its freshness and acquire undesirable flavors. In his opinion, the peculiar taste of aluminum cans and the inconvenience of lugging empty bottles back to the liquor store further reinforced his preference for draft beer at home. He also celebrated that he was saving at least 50% because those taverns were making a fortune. He ignored that his beer consumption at home more than quadrupled when he occasionally stopped for a cold one on his way home. In his mind, he justified that having a keg in the garage was tastier and thriftier. I couldn't have agreed more since I wasn't old enough to stop at a tavern. I never voiced this out loud.

Having a cold, frothy beer in his slippers by the fireplace was the epitome of relaxation for him. As a young college student, I couldn't care less about the intricacies of beer flavor. Beer was simply beer to me. Nonetheless, the thrill of sneaking a few bottles or cans from my father's stash was not without its risks. The man was vigilant, and I knew he could count his inventory. The new pour-on-demand system proved to be my perfect clandestine source of underage alcohol. With a stash of plastic cups conveniently located beside the refrigerator, I could quickly grab a quick beer now and then.

Returning home from college on occasional weekends or holidays, I no longer had to worry about finding someone twenty-one to purchase alcohol for me illegally. It was all right there in my garage, waiting to be consumed. However, an issue arose during my summer break. Not only did I frequent the garage for an occasional beer or two, but my friends also began to drop by more frequently for beer-fueled gatherings. With my stay-at-home mother rarely venturing into the garage, we were virtually unsupervised, leading to a summer filled with endless suds and laughter.

One day, as the beer delivery guy arrived with a new keg, my father unexpectedly returned home. I was in the garage with the delivery guy when my father confronted him about delivering half-empty kegs. The delivery guy vehemently insisted that the kegs were always full upon delivery.

Unfazed, my father retrieved a small notebook where he had meticulously recorded every beer consumed since the last delivery. Armed with his calculations, he revealed that a half keg should contain 15.5 gallons, equivalent to 165 12-ounce beers. He presented the dates and quantities consumed, proving the last keg yielded only 7 gallons. He had even figured in a generous spillage allowance. The delivery guy, only a few years older than me, exchanged a knowing glance with me but remained silent. He reassured my father that the kegs were properly filled, emphasizing that he would have noticed a lighter keg since he lifted them all day. Making a note to report back to his boss, the delivery guy left. And just like that, my 'summer of suds' came to an abrupt and sobering end.

Father B.

My grandparents had a unique mixed-religion marriage in 1917. My grandfather George Young's family roots were deep in the Methodist church. His grandfathcr donated the land for the M.E church in my hometown back in the 1820s. My grandmother Rose (nee Lampe) Young's family was staunch Roman Catholics from Germany. George and Rose's marriage was solemnized in the priest's home before mass on a Sunday morning. Neither of their parents were in attendance. The only people to attend the wedding were their siblings. Despite this unconventional beginning to their marriage, they made it work their entire lives. He would drop her off at her church on the way to his services and pick her up afterward at St Joe's after she attended mass.

My parents weren't religious and didn't attend church regularly, but my grandmother made a valiant attempt to expose me to Catholicism. As a small child, I was dressed up in a red blazer and bowtie and taken with her to every church service and event possible. I guess she thought I would absorb religion by exposure. My grandmother struggled to keep me still during the long Catholic service, and I would often escape her control and create chaos throughout the building. Remember, this was back when Latin was still the primary language in mass, so nothing was likely to soak into my head.

As you will see, I developed a special relationship with Father B., the long-time parish priest, during the 1950s-60s. In the back of the church were racks of votive candles that people would light for prayer intentions. As a child, I loved playing with matches and would beg my grandmother to let me go back to light some candles. She would always cave in and let me go. One day, Fr B. caught me blowing out candles already lit by other parishioners. He had a long talk with my grandmother, ending that little diversion during Mass. My grandmother also explained the concept of Catholic mortal sins to me. She said a gravely sinful act could lead to eternal damnation if a person does not repent the sin before death. She always used the phrase "Going to Hell in a Handbasket" when trying to control me. She terrified me, so whenever I misbehaved, she told me that it was a mortal sin and that I needed to shape up. I still feel uneasy about turning around in a church pew, even if it is not a Catholic church.

As an adult, my neighbor, who owned the local bowling alley, told me numerous stories of my childhood escapades during services where Father B wasn't happy with my behavior. When you enter the church, you first see fonts filled with holy water blessed by the priest for people to dip their fingers in. It is a symbol of the sacrament of baptism. Father B caught me running loose from my grandmother multiple times when I played in these fonts, splashing water around. Yes, it is another mortal sin still on my list.

My grandmother always sat in the same pew, third from the front on the left side on the aisle. I was to sit right next to her and not move. So, I was always front and center for everyone to witness my behavior. Asperges is the rite of sprinkling the altar, clergy, and congregation with holy water before mass. I made it a game of trying to avoid Father B splashing me with Holy Water like I was a vampire. I would hide behind my grandmother or duck under the pew as Fr. B came down the aisle. I was told that one time when I was hiding under the pew, Fr. B knelt to make sure he dosed me multiple times. The whole congregation burst out laughing. Yep, another mortal sin. We are going to need a larger handbasket.

Ash Wednesday one year was another clash with Fr B. I went with my grandmother to this service to mark the beginning of Lent. When it was time for her to get in line to receive her mark, she took me up front rather than leave me alone in the pew. Who knows what I might have done? As Fr. B was coming down the line marking everyone with the ashes of the palm fronds forming a cross, I thought this would look cool on my forehead. I didn't know you had to be confirmed in the church to receive this sacrament. So, as grandmother got her ashes and stood up from kneeling, Fr B passed me by and went on to the next person in line. I stood up with my hands on my hips and loudly yelled, "Hey, I want some dirt on my forehead." Fr. B just smiled, made the sign of the cross at me, and moved on. Yes, I now had a rather lengthy list of kid mortal sins.

My grandmother always took me to fundraising festivals at her church and neighboring towns. I did enjoy that part of the church. Lots of food and rides for kids, plus only a few things I could get in trouble doing. One year at the festival, I discovered they had a blackjack card game in our church basement. My grandmother loved playing cards and taught me how to play '21' very well. I hopped into an open seat and discovered that Fr. B was the dealer. He and I looked at each other like in a scene from Seinfeld, Fr. B seemed to say, "Hello, Newman." I explained to him that I knew how to play and had money. I was dealt my hand and had 12, so I shouted, "Hit Me, Father, Hit Me" The table exploded in laughter. I didn't understand. My grandmother soon found me; it was time to leave the church bazaar. I was just beginning to have fun.

I was staying at my grandparents' house one weekend when Fr. B came to their door. At first, I thought I had gotten caught doing something again. My five-year-old brain was very relieved when I heard Fr. B and Grandma discussing the church school building fund. Quickly their voices got louder as an argument developed. Fr. B started yelling at my grandmother, demanding she give more money. I heard Father B say something that upset me: "If you don't give more, you are going to Hell." I started crying and started begging my grandmother to please give more money. "I don't want you to go to Hell in a handbasket." My grandmother was in tears and very upset; the priest was red in the face and yelling when my stoic Methodist grandfather calmly stepped into the conversation. He handed Fr. B his hat and pointed to the door, telling him it was time to leave. This was the only time I ever saw them discuss religion.

Years later, as a young adult, I was at River Downs horse track in Cincinnati with some friends. I noticed an old guy standing at the rail by himself and finally recognized it was Fr. B in civilian clothing. Memories of him yelling at my grandmother began to flood back. It was time to confront this guy. I went up to him standing there; he had a wad of race tickets in one hand with a drink in the other while smoking a large stinky cigar. I introduced myself; he had no idea who I was. It took a while, but I finally got him to remember my grandmother dragging me to church in the red blazer. When the light bulb finally went on who I was, I reminded him of the church building fund scene, yelling at my grandmother and making her cry. I told him, "So, Father B, did you not bring the wife with you to the track." He started yelling at me about the insinuation, and I said, "Look at you, standing there with all your sins of smoking, drinking, and gambling." "Who is going to Hell, now." My grandmother's religious training about mortal sins was finally put into use. She would have been proud, but I still have this irrational fear of small wicker baskets.

My Favorite High School Teacher

We all have favorite teachers; I was lucky to have several terrific educators who tried to impart their wisdom to me. My most unforgettable teacher was a sweet little lady from Havana, Cuba. In the mid-1960s, Yolanda Piñeiro fled her Cuban homeland to escape the Fidel Castro regime with little more than a suitcase. She arrived in Miami with her Ph.D. in Education from the University of Havana and her adult daughter and elderly mother. She told us how it was a big treat to have enough money (5 cents) for a single White Castle sandwich for her meal of the day. Somehow, she landed in the middle of the United States farm country teaching Spanish in Shelbyville, Indiana, high school. I am eternally grateful that she did.

Yolanda Pinero

Due to the crazy US/Cuban politics of the time, our US government would not recognize her education credentials, a Ph.D. from the University of Havana: Foreign Language Dept. Academics. Yolanda attended Cornell University, earning a B.S. and then an M.A. from Ball State to get her US-approved teaching credentials.

I had to take a foreign language to be on the college prep track, so in the 9th grade, I signed up for Spanish. I had a lovely American lady teaching Spanish 1 during my freshman year. I can't remember her name or much about the classes she taught. I vividly remember the first day of Spanish 2 when this tiny lady with a beautiful Cuban accent introduced herself to our class. She was maybe 4' 8" feet tall and maybe half that wide with tiny little legs, always wearing chunky high-heeled shoes; she looked like a sparrow. I can't remember what she said, but I was captivated and took Spanish for four years in high school. I was probably her worst student for Spanish pronunciation. I can still hear her chuckling as I struggled with speaking. "Oh Jorge, wat hoppens to ewe." I eventually became pretty good at translating written and spoken Spanish, but I could not eliminate my Hoosier Spanglish accent.

One vivid memory of her class was about me trying to impress Yolanda before the Christmas holiday break in my junior year. I wrote her a note in Spanish and ended it with a holiday greeting, or so I thought. Most of you know my English grammar and punctuation could be better. Well, you guessed it, in Spanish, it was the same. I can't remember what I wrote in the note that I translated into Spanish. I ended my note to her with 'Feliz y Próspero Ano Nuevo.' One Spanish accent mark is called a "tilde." In English, a "tilde" refers to the "mustache" that goes over the "n" (ñ).

When Mrs. P read my note, she burst into uncontrollable laughter. I didn't think I had written anything funny, but she was crying with laughter, and she said, "Jorge, you must work on your Spanish punctuation." She explained while wiping tears from her eyes to me that año with the tilde meant 'year' and ano without the tilde meant 'anus.' She said no one had ever wished her a happy and prosperous new butt hole before. Boy, was I mortified.

Mrs. P sponsored our extracurricular Spanish Club, which met once a month during our activity period. When I was a senior, the Spanish Club had grown to 65 members. Annual Christmas fiestas were held, and guest speakers frequently attended. The most unusual aspect of the club was our fundraising for college scholarships. Other groups like the 'band geeks' got to sell delicious candy bars to buy uniforms. Being one of the newer clubs left us with the unique opportunity of selling combs and toothbrushes door to door. Yes, that was a tough sell, but I happily accepted a $25 scholarship at the end of my senior year.

Like kids often do, we liked to find ways to sidetrack/derail our teacher's lesson plans. Yolanda was easy to distract, or so we thought at the time. We would find ways to ask her about Fidel Castro; she was very passionately against him and his regime. You could see her face flush red, and she would abandon her lesson plan on verb conjugation of irregular future tense. We didn't realize she told these stories in English and partly Spanish. We were learning Spanish via conversation plus firsthand Cuban history. Priceless!

One story that has stuck with me for decades was when Yolanda was a student at the University of Havana at the same time as Fidel. She told us he was a brilliant law student yet an arrogant show-off with a photographic memory. One day in the student commons, he sat at a table smoking his large signature cigar while reading his law books. He would read a page, rip it out of the book, light it from his cigar, and then repeat it verbatim. Fidel was famous for giving hours-long speeches from memory. He didn't use notes to read from, and they didn't have teleprompters back then.

Mrs. P left Cuba when Fidel banned religion. She always said Fidel wasn't a communist at heart but was power-hungry. Her husband was the Havana District Attorney; he chose to remain in Cuba under Fidel's rule. It's a tiny world; in the 1990s, I was hiking in the PNW with a friend whose parents had also fled Cuba. I told him about Mrs. P.

He mentioned that his father had been a defense attorney in Havana. When he got back from our hike, he called his dad in Miami and asked if he, by chance, knew the Pineros. Not only did he know them, but they also used to party together. It truly is a small world.

Mrs. P didn't just teach us the language but made sure we got the cultural aspects of Cuban life. During my senior year, our 4th-year Spanish class gathered at one of our classmates' homes one weekend for a Cuban meal cooked by Mrs. P. She fixed a colossal feast of 'arroz con pollo Cubano' (chicken and rice). It differed significantly from our everyday Hoosier Sunday fried chicken meal our grandma made. Many new flavors were introduced to us. We also got to use our Spanish around the dinner table.

Yolanda and Piñata

If we had been good, productive students, Mrs. P would have given us several games to play in Spanish as a break from conjugating verbs. One of those games was called Loteria, like Bingo but with Spanish words instead of numbers. Mrs. P would call out words, and we would cover them on our cards and shout out LOTERIA when we got the line covered.

One unusual thing she did as a punishment would threaten disruptive students with her infamous "red dot" in her grade book. Because red symbolized communism and Fidel, she felt that was the worst thing she could do to you. She always had good control of her classroom, plus this threat was so different from that of other teachers; it was a very effective technique to get the students' attention. I don't think I ever got a red dot, but maybe I should have. I will let you decide.

I took a fourth year of Spanish because she made her classes enjoyable. I had no aspirations for using the language since I lived in a tiny town in Indiana. It was an elective that was not needed to fulfill any HS graduation requirements or prerequisites for college. The class was very small, with only 6 or 7 students, so we got personalized intensive instruction. If I don't say so myself, our language skills improved tremendously.

Mrs. P. obtained enough copies in Spanish of a short 17th-century novel written by Miguel de Cervantes. He wrote the classic 'Don Quixote de la Mancha,' the adventure novel about a crazy Spanish knight. Cervantes also wrote many other novels, short stories, poems, and plays. I can't remember the title of the novel we read, but the main character was named Ignacio. Mrs. P would assign the class pages each day to have us translate and read out loud in Spanish the next day. We had to be prepared because she randomly called us to do a page. It wasn't five days a week since she had other activities and lessons to do. The book was written in Spanish Castilian style from the 17th century, so it would be comparable to Shakespearian English of the same era compared to American English. It differed from the Spanish spoken in Latin America, adding an additional challenge.

We started this novel in the second half of our senior year. We all adored Mrs. P., but she was pushing us pretty hard.

We all had the standard case of senioritis. The self-opinion of our academic abilities was high, and yes, our egos were getting too big for our britches. Nothing added to our permanent records cards at this point would affect graduation or college admissions. I hate to admit it, but I initiated a scheme to cut down our volume of homework. I didn't think of it as cheating but more of a homework evasion system.

Usually, Mrs. P. would assign about five pages of the novel, which might take an hour or so to translate each night. Since there were just a few of us in the class, I planned for each of us to do one page. I grabbed a box of carbon paper from my dad's office. For you youngsters, this was thin paper coated with a mixture of wax and pigment used between two sheets of ordinary paper to make one or more copies of an original document. Normally this was for a typewriter, but it will work the same for handwriting if you press hard on your pen. I planned for us to write one page and make copies for the others in the class. Each day in the hallway after class, I would assign each co-conspirator pages they were responsible for completing. Everyone was ecstatic about cutting down on the homework; we had critical Senior things like prom and graduation to think about.

Each day before class started, we would exchange our translations, giving each a complete set for the daily homework assignment. Yes, the handwriting differed on each page, but we didn't turn them in but merely recited our translations. We all had excellent translation skills, even if my pronunciation was sketchy. The plan was working to perfection until one of the cogs in our conspiracy called in sick one day. Four students had four pages of five pages, and we were all missing the 3rd page.

Mrs. P called on me to read that 3rd page, and I said I was sorry but unable to translate it. She said, 'No, Problemo Jorge,' and called on another classmate to read page 3, who also said they could not translate. Mrs. P started walking around the room and said nothing at first, and then she asked a third student who likewise was unable to give her a translation. Mrs. P was silent and didn't say a word. She moved on to pages four and five and completed the daily assignment. Whoop, that was close. We had not counted on anyone being absent.

Before class ended, Mrs. P gave us the next assignment, seven pages. I divvied up the pages and called the sick student that night, who said they would return the next day. No problem. The next day we could recite our translations for all seven pages. Mrs. P smiled and looked pleased with our progress.

That day she increased the next assignment to ten pages, telling us we were doing a good job and that she wanted to pick up the pace so we could finish the book sooner. 'No Problemo,' that is only two pages each vs. the five we were doing. We were still working on the plan. Before we knew it, she had increased the number of pages daily to 25. The logistics were getting crazy trying to assemble the pages and read before we had to recite the translations.

Mrs. P had figured out our ploy and had not said a word. Her revenge was not turning us in for cheating but to make us work even harder. It took us longer to figure out her retaliation than it took her to discover our deceit. We finally confessed and apologized. She returned to the normal original pace. The smartass full of ourselves seniors thought we were so much shrewder than our willy veteran educator. We learned a big lesson in this scheme, which wasn't Spanish. Thanks, Mrs. P.

It wasn't too many years after I graduated from high school that Mrs. P retired from teaching. She moved to New York to live with her daughter. She kept in contact with her fellow teachers who remained in town so that we would get occasional updates from her from them. They all traveled together and remained friends for a long time.

I continued my Spanish education at Indiana University; I was required to take two semesters of a foreign language for the degree I was pursuing. I tested into Level 3 but decided to take Level 2 classes to ease into college with a couple of "bunny" classes. HA.

My first instructor was an older gentleman who spoke no English, his first name was Zdenek, and his second name was at least fifteen consonants and no vowels. He told us in Spanish not to try to pronounce his last name and that he was a refugee from the Czechoslovakian Soviet invasion of 1968. That was the extent of our first class, learning his name and that he was very new to the United States. He spoke a Castilian Spanish dialect very different from the Cuban dialect Mrs. P taught me in high school. He was supposed to teach us a predetermined departmental course that would be tested and graded by the department at the end of the semester. Zdenek was a very nice man in a foreign country trying to recover from being uprooted from his homeland. One day another student and I took him to a grocery store so he could learn how things worked here in the US. The class went well, and it was time for our departmental final. Nothing he taught us was on the exam; Gracias a Dios for Mrs. P's lessons from high school saved my ass. The class in which I hoped to get an 'Easy 4.0' turned into a 3.0.

The second semester I got a young Austrian woman who

spoke seven languages and wasn't shy about correcting my Hoosier into English. Much to my chagrin, this class was not grammar but Spanish poetry and literature. This was my weakest subject in English, and now I have an Austrian instructing me about Spanish literature. OH My, what happened to my easy bunny classes? To top it off, this was a 7:30 AM class. As I said, poetry, in general, escaped me. One poem she assigned confounded me; I spent a long time translating it into English before I tried to understand the deeper meaning of the author's words. It was just random words; I was frustrated and had no clue. That evening, some dormitory buddies and I somehow stumbled onto a case of beer. The next day, with an intense hangover, I made it to class. The smug instructor asked us what we had learned about this poem. We all said it was beyond our comprehension. The instructor said she was friends with the poet, who was experimenting with a new art form without hidden meaning. This didn't sit well with my hangover, and I stormed out of class, muttering. Hello, I received a 2.0 grade, which I originally planned to get a 4.0.

This ended my Spanish academic career, but the great memories of Mrs. P have stayed with me for a long time. Gracias Senora Piñeiro!

Grandpa George

I don't remember a time that I didn't know that I was named after my grandfather, George Elliot Young. I was George Eric Young, so we almost had identical names. We were still both George E. Young. I was his first grandchild and carried his name. He was extra proud, and I certainly felt his love. The story was that when I was born, he was so excited that he wanted to record my birth certificate personally, but he was so enthusiastic that he filled out the form with my name as George Egbert Young, not George Eric Young. Thank God that the error was corrected in time. Egbert would have been a horrible burden on the school playground.

George & Georgie

Grandpa George helped instill my free-range spirit from an early age. He continuously surprised me with things to do together on the spur of the moment. He would often show up at my house, and we would go for an adventure. He probably wanted to be a fireman. Our town fire department had a system of bells that would ring when a fire broke out. The number of rings would signal to the volunteer firemen in their homes what section of town a fire was located so they could report directly to the fire rather than gather at the fire station. My grandfather would often listen for the bells and come to get me so we could watch the firemen put out the blaze. He would drop whatever he was doing at work, and we would "chase" the fire. Riding in the car's front seat, I would look for smoke to help direct us to the exact location.

One day, he arrived excited to get to a massive grain elevator fire across from the Porter swimming pool. The fire department had called in extra fire engines from neighboring towns. We couldn't drive closer than a couple of city blocks, but we could see the flames shooting high into the sky. We walked to get closer to the fire. I could feel the heat even far away. When we returned the next day, the firemen were still putting out the hot spots. The remaining skeleton of the building was eerie.

Another spur-of-the-moment thing Grandpa George would do is show up unannounced to take me fishing. Since he owned his own company, I was curious if he just got done early or got fed up and needed a break. He always wore a white shirt with sleeve garters and a tie at work, which he would wear to go fishing. I saw him mowing his grass in that same outfit. Thinking back, I don't remember if he had casual work clothes. He is wearing a tie in all the pictures I have of him. It didn't matter to me; going with him to another secret fishing hole he would tell me about as we drove there was always a great treat. His favorite fishing gear was a simple bamboo cane pole with a short line, bobber, and sinker. These poles would be lashed to the top of his car since they were so long. We would often stop at bait shops where he would talk to the shop owners about what the hot bait was at the time: nightcrawlers, minnows, mealworms, etc.

Sometimes, we planned fishing trips where I would stay overnight and take off early in the mornings. The night before, he showed me how to flood an area in his yard with the hose and come back after dark with a flashlight to scoop up the biggest nightcrawlers. We would head out a few times without any bait, which confused me. It turned out he knew the fish were biting on crawdad's tails. If you didn't know, crawdads or crayfish are freshwater crustaceans resembling small lobsters. We first had to fish for crawdads in the shoreline, and he would pinch their tails off and use that for bait. Crazy crawdads would grab ahold of the bare hook. I was always scared of touching them or getting pinched but catching them was fun.

Little Clam Lake - 1958

Grandpa once took Grandma and me to Wisconsin to stay in a cabin on a chain of small lakes for a week. I still remember the name of the lake, Little Clam Lake, located in the northern part of the state, almost next to Lake Superior. There were no interstates back then, so it took several days of driving to get there. He told me we would be fishing from a boat instead of the bank, so I would need to learn how to use a baitcasting reel. I would go to their house, sit in the backyard, and set targets to perfect my casting technique. This lake had panfish and muskies. Walleyes and bass. Previously all we had fished for were panfish like crappies, sunfish, bluegill, etc. Grandpa said we needed to use "plugs" for the bigger fish. I was shocked to learn plugs were not something alive but a hardwood/plastic body with treble hooks hanging from it. They supposedly mimicked bait fish the larger fish fed upon. I was hooked, more than once, on those treble hooks during practices. They were more than a bit of ouchy.

We arrived at Little Clam Lake and found our camp, which rented cabins and boats. Grandpa and Grandma started unpacking the car. I grabbed my pole that had a lure rigged and raced to the dock to practice my casting. I had been couped up in a car for two days and needed something to do. I think it was my second cast that something unexpected happened….. Zzzziiiiiiinnnnnnggggg…….. the line on my reel started flying out, I tried like crazy to set the drag tighter, but I couldn't stop it. I was frozen, and then the end of the line was reached. Zap. Whatever I had hooked was long gone. My grandfather came running; I thought I was in trouble for losing the lure and all that line. I was wrong; he carried another pole and was casting himself. Back at the car, my grandmother yelled, "Come unload the car. There's plenty of time to fish later." That was my first "you should have seen how big the one was that got away" story.

It was a great week of fishing. We went fishing in the rowboat outfitted with a small outboard engine twice daily. I learned how to start and operate the boat, which was as fun as fishing. The camp offered a fish cleaning service, so we didn't have to do that yucky part of fishing. They would filet and freeze our catch every day. My grandpa said we should concentrate on the panfish to fill his freezer for the winter. I am telling you, these panfish were enormous, almost the size of a dinner plate. It was all a six-year-old could do to reel them into the boat. We would usually fill up a couple of stringers left dangling over the side of the boat, then head back to the dock. One day the fishing had been excellent, and the stringers were overflowing; I caught the last fish and was struggling to hold this fish in one hand and unhook the stringer with the other. I lost my grip on the stringer and watched the fish slowly swim away. It was sad knowing all those fish were lost. The next day we went back to that spot because the fishing was so good, and we found the stringer floating with just the fish heads; it appeared that the turtles had a feast. I learned a hard lesson. Hold on tightly to the stringer full of fish.

The cabin had a small kitchen, but my grandmother declared loudly that she was on vacation, so we ate every night at local restaurants. Breakfast was cereal, and lunch was cold-cut sandwiches. She never went fishing in the boat with us but occasionally would fish off the dock. Overall, it was a great trip, fishing all day with my grandpa, pitching horseshoes in the evening, and listening to the other cabins talking about the ones that got away. One day we watched wild rice (Manoomin), a cereal grain harvested by natives in canoes using sticks to knock the rice grain into the bottom of the canoe. It grows along the shallow edges of the lakes. Are the fish still biting on Little Clam Lake?

Shelby County Fair - 1954

The Shelby County Fair was a big deal when I was a kid. It had rides for kids, 4H barns with animals, horse racing, and food vendors. My grandfather owned a company, Young Oil and Supply. He owned many service stations and delivered home heating oil throughout Shelby County. Every year he had a large tent at the fair. He loved staying in the tent and talking to people. My grandmother said he would practically sleep there so he wouldn't miss a moment. They had a robot made from Phillips 66 oil cans with arms that moved. It also talked to me when I visited; I later learned it was my grandpa with a microphone from the back of the tent.

My grandfather was quiet, and I never remember him talking about his family. I became interested in genealogy in my forties and have discovered much about his past. I wish I had asked more questions back then. I have learned a lot about him and his family after I left the area and moved to the Pacific Northwest. George quit high school when his father died. He became the family wage earner to support his mother and younger brother. His first job was with a company less than a block from his house, the Index Notion company, a 5 & 10 department store. He was a quick study rising quickly to be the manager. He even traveled to other cities as the company grew. In 1922 he was appointed as postmaster in Shelbyville by President Harding. He stayed postmaster until 1935 when he started Young Oil Company.

Doing my genealogy research, I learned that the land of the County fairgrounds was part of the Young family's 1822 homestead. I am confident his enthusiasm for hanging out in the tent at the county fair was partly connected with his family heritage, yet he never spoke of it. I now know his favorite fishing holes that we fished were located on that family farm. It has taken me many decades to learn what he taught me about the family without mentioning it. It makes my memories even more special as I continue to uncover these pieces to the family puzzle.

In 1954 the General Electric company came to town and built a large factory. One day my grandfather picked me up as he often did for our surprise adventures. He said we were going to a groundbreaking. I had no clue what this meant, but we had shovels in the car. Digging and playing in the dirt sounded like great fun. We drove to the edge of town and parked on the edge of this large field. There were many men with hard hats, shovels, and a sign with a big G. E. in the middle of the sign. I was only four, but I knew those were my and grandpa's initials. I was impressed by all those people gathered to honor my grandfather and me by digging in the dirt with us. It was such a great feeling to be the center of attention. A guy with a camera had us line up to take our picture. My grandfather said it would be in the newspaper. WOW

Another great adventure my grandpa George took me on was going to a Chicago White Sox game to see them play the New York Yankees in 1955. The trip started by taking my first train ride. I had been to the train station many times before with my grandpa because his cousin was the station master. While my grandpa was chatting with his cousin, I would play with the wagons and carts used to load and unload the freight. Sometimes a train would arrive, and I saw people get on and off.

The Riley

The "Riley," as it was also known, hit the rails in the early 1940s during the first years of the streamliner age. It sported a sleek look that included a shrouded steam locomotive. The James Whitcomb Riley was one of many regional services the New York Central provided between its larger cities. This train served the Chicago - Cincinnati market via Indianapolis, running over the famed "Big Four Route." The 214-mile trip from Shelbyville to Chicago Central Station at Michigan Ave & Roosevelt Road took about 5 hours. The train ride was excellent; we got to eat breakfast and watch the countryside go by, but I mostly slept since it was very early in the morning departure.

We took my first cab ride from the train station to Comiskey Park. The baseball stadium was so large that I was in awe. The crowd was huge, but somehow, we found our seats on the first base side behind the Yankee's dugout. We weren't in the first section of box seats next to the field but not the nosebleed seats. I was close enough to be sure the players could hear me cheer them. I brought my mitt to snag an errant fly ball, which proved unnecessary. My first in-person big league ball game and Mickey Mantle hit a home run. I was cheering like crazy when he entered the dugout after rounding the bases. The crowd and I continued to cheer so loud that he came back out of the dugout to see me giving him a standing ovation; he took off his cap, smiled, and pointed right at me. Mickey pointed right at me.

I didn't know it then, but that homerun was one for the record books. On Sunday, June 5th, 1955, Mickey Mantle batting right-handed, hit his 97th homerun over the roof in left field 550' off Chicago Billy Pierce, bounced onto 34th street, and broke a car window. It was a doubleheader that day, and Grandpa said he wanted to stay, but we would miss the train back home. The game was great, so I didn't mind missing the second game; I don't remember exactly what foods I ate, but I am sure my grandfather would not have turned down any request for what the vendors were hawking in the stands. I am sure I got it all by asking for cotton candy, hot dogs, popcorn, and cracker jack.

So, I remember being exhausted and stuffed when the game was over; I am surprised I didn't barf. My baseball hero hit a home run, and now it was time to head back to Shelbyville, Indiana, from the big city of Chicago. The buildings were huge, and so many people. A lot different from the small town I grew up in. We reversed the trip, took a cab ride back to the train station, and waited for the Riley. I don't remember the train trip back, but I remember Grandpa carrying me to his car to take me home. What a great day! I spent the day with my heroes, Mickey Mantle and Grandpa George.

Grandpa George was always very good to his employees; at Christmas time, they rented a room at a nice restaurant to hold an employee Christmas party where they would get an envelope with some cash. I always got to go and was usually just the only kid. One year they did allow kids, and Santa showed up with presents. I remember going to nearby towns to fancy places, well fancy to me, one of those was the Durbin Hotel in Rushville. The Durbin was famous for being the unofficial headquarters of Wendell Willkie's presidential campaign. Another year I remember going to the Blue Bird in Morristown, renowned for its fried chicken. He always had such a great smile while talking to his employees at these affairs.

I don't remember Grandpa drinking often, but his drink of choice was an 'old fashion.' Today I occasionally order an 'old fashion,' and the aroma brings back vivid memories. Strangely, I can't remember his voice, but a whiff of a properly made drink with cherries, an orange slice, and a dash of bitters with a generous jigger of whisky can trigger great images and thoughts. My grandfather didn't drink at home because my grandmother disapproved, but he kept a bottle of whisky in the cupboard in case of a nasty cough. (cough-cough)

On Christmas Eve, he would invite his employees to stop by his home for a Christmas eggnog. He would make the eggnog himself and be very liberal with the spirits. I stayed there one year for Christmas Eve and got to observe. My grandmother always disapproved yet let this go on because my grandfather said it was good for the company's morale. One employee would show up, and they would sit in the living room and chat for a bit, having their Christmas cheer. Then another employee would show up, and this ritual was repeated. Pretty soon, it was a crowd. I noticed my grandma's displeasure, she was banging the dishes around in the kitchen, but she never voiced it. Looking back, I am sure my grandfather gave each employee a different time to arrive. He was pretty lit by the time the last employee left.

I have great memories of Grandpa George and try to emulate him daily. He instilled in me a sense of adventure that helped foster my free-range childhood.

Bus Money Scam

Like many of my youth stories, this also involves scamming money for snacks. In my first four years of grade school, I walked to school even though it was ten miles, uphill hill, both directions through snow up to my waist. It was only four city blocks on flat terrain. Our schools were very crowded; the baby boomers were straining the school systems. My first-grade class had 35 kids. Like other primary schools, it was very crowded. When I was in the fifth grade, we moved from a house in the city built in 1890 to a brand-new house in the suburbs. Many new homes were being built then, and a new school was planned within walking distance of these new additions. However, it wouldn't be finished for another year. So, for my fifth year, I was transferred to another older primary school closer to my house. It was about a mile and a half from our new house. All the schools in town were within walking distance of the students, but this was determined to be too far, so the school system provided bus transportation for a fee. Kids could purchase a bus ticket at school that the bus driver would punch as they got on the bus. This one bus traveled to all the outlying areas of town, picking up kids living in the far corners of the districts considered not within average walking distance. This was because of all the uphill snow conditions in both directions.

The only problem was that it added a lot of time to my school day. I had to be ready 45 minutes earlier in the morning to ride the bus. That was a major issue since I was almost a teenager and needed extra sleep time. Problem solved: the neighbor across the street gave me, a few other kids, and his cute daughter a ride to school on his way to work. The neighborhood kids and I were understood to ride the bus home after school. We had to wait in a classroom for about 45 minutes after school for this bus to show up and eventually drop us off in our neighborhood. We were not allowed to wait in front of the school or on the playground but under the watchful eye of a stern teacher. This was killing me. Being in a classroom all day was bad enough, but the extra imprisonment time was torture.

I planned to bust out of this bogus incarceration; I told my teacher that my grandparents lived a few blocks away. That was the truth, but I may have failed to mention to the teacher that I was not going to their house but walked home instead. Leaving when school was over, I could walk a mile and a half home, beat the bus dropping kids off, and have little time to screw around along the way. I was a healthy ten-year-old boy with energy to burn, and the exercise was good for me. Being cooped up in the classroom was so boring; my plan was spectacular. My mother was always surprised when I came home soaking wet after riding the bus.

I was a happy camper walking outdoors, not constricted to an empty classroom with nothing to do. In hindsight, I could have done my homework, but that was off my radar. One night at dinner, my dad asked, "Don't you need money for the bus?" Ding Ding Ding, a giant lightbulb went off in my head. Why had I not thought about this before now? "Yes, I certainly do need bus money! Thanks for reminding me." I made a mental note to ask once a week for 'bus money.'

Two neighborhood grocery stores along my route home had terrific candy displays and a chest cooler with ten flavors of soda pop. Since I got a ride in the morning and was walking home at night, this 'bus money' became a great source of disposable income. I was happy to dispose of it at these fine local merchant establishments. I was doing my part to help the local economy. These places were hangouts for kids, so I got to socialize for a while before I had to hit the trail and trek homeward.

I always kept a bus ticket with a few punches remaining in my wallet in case the weather was too bad or I was tired. Like clockwork, once a week or so, I would hit the old man up for more 'bus money.' A few times, I would ask for money out of the normal cycle trying to increase my pocket change, until one day, the old man got suspicious and started asking questions. My mom spilled the beans on my morning ride to school. The jig was up; I had to acknowledge the conspiracy of not riding the bus and using the ill-gotten gains for candy and soda. Despite all my best logic, my endeavors to get out of this jam failed. I was in deep trouble.

This was the only time in history that a kid had ever been grounded for getting more exercise than his parents had expected. When that school year ended, the new grade school just a short walk from my house was finally completed, thus ending the need to ride the bus to my 6th grade. The irony is that the following year, for middle school, I was expected to get to junior high school, which is located a few blocks from the 5th-grade class. I secured a ten-speed bicycle to become my transportation for middle school, but that is a story for another day.

Reunion Switcheroo

My oldest friend, Darryl Curson, sent me this picture, circa 1953/4, from his picture vault. I am on the far right with Darryl to my left, then his brothers Farell and Alan in their backyard. 'Darry,' as I called him back then, and I was constantly having adventures. You can read about them in his book, The St. Mary Street Kids: A Childhood Memoir by Darryl Curson, available on Amazon. Darryl and I lived across the street from each other since we were two; we went to grade school, junior high, High School, and college together. After graduation, we started our careers and drifted apart, eventually moving away from our hometowns but keeping in touch now and then.

After our retirement, we started having more frequent contact on Facebook, mostly centered around our weird humor. Despite living 2000 miles apart, we started collaborating on several joint projects. Off Their Rockers is a daily cartoon we publish on Facebook, plus we have produced several cartoon and humor books with several on the drawing board. Darryl is the artist. I remember a box that held one of our parents' new refrigerators that became a space rocket decorated mainly by Darryl.

We also always saw each other at class reunions. One year I

believe it was at our 20th HS reunion, the St Mary Street Boys pulled off one of our most incredible adventures. Darryl and I were not physical twins in any fashion except that we both had dark hair and wore black horn-rimmed glasses like we did in high school at that point. This year we arrived at the reunion hall at the same time. While standing in line to check in, we devised a plan to have fun as we did as kids. After twenty years nobody looked like they did in high school, so we decided to switch name tags that had our high school graduation picture and would pretend to be each other.

The entire evening was terrific talking to fellow classmates about the good old days while pretending to be the other person. We knew each other's family and work history well enough to carry on decent conversations with our inebriated classmates. It wasn't until the end of the evening when Darryl and I were standing next to each other when a very drunk classmate said, "Hey, wait a minute, something is not right" He was pointing to me and said, "You aren't Darryl" The jig was up. The St. Mary Street Boys pulled off another great adventure.

This stunt had become a legend. At our 50th reunion, people asked for ID before talking to us, remembering our shenanigans 30 years prior. For our 65th reunion, we can probably do it again. I hope we cannot forget to pull off the "Old Switcheroo" one more time.

Teenage Boy Behavior

I remember my mind and body changing in middle school. I grew almost a foot taller in the 7th grade. Changing from a boy to a young man was quite perplexing. I don't think I was mentally aware of these changes back then. There is a reason they separate middle school children from grade school and high school. It's more of a containment than a separation. Trying to educate this age group is useless. I do remember strange behavior changes starting when I was in junior high school.

Our lunchroom was on the bottom floor of the school. We all lined up through the cafeteria for our nutritionally balanced, low-cost Type "A" meal. I remember the food being very bland and unappetizing, but I would hang around after inhaling my lunch and asking the lunch ladies if they had any leftovers. I had a bottomless pit for my stomach.

While hanging out in the hallways after the feeding frenzy, the boys would say mean things to our buddies that we didn't mean, and the girls would say nice things to their friends they didn't mean. We, boys, would also punch each other in the arm at every opportunity to impress the girls with how tough we were while at the same time trying to avoid getting Cooties from the girls. It was a very confusing and bewildering time.

Making a circle with thumbs and the first finger was a stupid game we played. The goal is not to look at this hand sign. If you do, you're bound to get sucker-punched, which nobody wanted. Want it to go away? You must try to stick your index finger in the hole — without looking at it. Doing this before you punched your best buddy for no reason was also unnecessary. I won't even go into the game of squirrel where boys punch each other in the nards.

After lunch, during inclement weather, which was most of the school year in Indiana, we would hang around the candy stand until it was time to return to classes. The student body made money off these sales. It was an excellent place to hang out, see, and be seen. It was also the scene of one of my many embarrassing teenage moments.

We had a minimum dress code at the time. Boys were supposed to wear shirts with a collar, and their shirttails had to be tucked into the pants. Girls had to wear dresses that had to touch the floor when they kneeled.

Gant was a popular brand of menswear that many boys started wearing in the 1960s. It supposedly was an Ivy League image with a 'locker loop.' A fabric loop is positioned high, usually where the pleat meets the yoke, in the center back of shirts. The purpose was to hang your shirt in a locker by the loop to prevent the shirt from wrinkling. They were more common on sports or Oxford button-down collar shirts. The loops soon started to symbolize a sort of high-status Ivy League fashion. Later, the loops became more a part of the collegiate culture. Other shirt brands followed the trend as their popularity grew.

The Locker Loop

The 'Locker Loop' was not considered 'cool' in our

midwestern farming community middle school. We all cut them off before going to school to avoid being teased about being uppity and pretentious. One day after lunch, I stood in the student commons area, arm punching and saying mean stuff to my buddies. I spotted a boy walking down the hallway wearing a crisp new shirt with a 'Locker Loop.' I didn't know this kid and can't remember his name. I ran down the hall after him and grabbed his 'Locker Loop' to yank it off. I was going to win the prize that day, Carpe Diem. Capturing this loop like the brass ring on the carousel at the county fair would make me a legend. I tugged with all my might after I got my finger secured in the loop. As I pulled, I ripped off the entire back of this poor kid's shirt. The loop didn't separate from the shirt as I imagined it was supposed to have done. I had the entire back of his shirt attached to my hand.

It was witnessed by hundreds of kids and a couple of teachers. Stunned by my actions, I heard a teacher yelling over the laughter, "Why did you rip his shirt off?" "Ummm, Ummmm, Ummm, I didn't mean to," I stammered. It was hard to deny that I tore his shirt when the evidence was hanging from my finger by the locker loop. I expected to have a prized, captured locker loop. Long story short, I had to explain to my parents that I needed some money to buy this kid another shirt.

The moral of the story is that Teenage Boys Do Dumb Stuff. I don't think we get wiser as we get older; we just run out of stupid stuff to do.

Grandma Rose's Bible

As a child, I remember always being fascinated by this huge old bible that my grandmother, Rose Lampe Young, often showed me. It was a huge leather-bound edition with ornate printing that must have been four or five inches thick. I am unsure if it was in English or German since I wasn't interested in the Bible. I was never allowed to touch it since it was old and fragile. The section I liked was blank pages with handwritten names and dates that seemed very mysterious. I eventually learned this was her family tree. She would show me different branches and tell me stories and dates about the people going back into her German family. These stories always fascinated me, but I didn't remember any details. I wish I had paid more attention to the details of her stories, as you will soon learn.

Grandma Rose & Georgie

Rose was very proud of her German Catholic heritage, so much so that I was under the impression that our entire family was German until I was in my forties and started doing our family genealogy. My grandfather was taciturn and never talked about his family history. I vaguely remember her talking about her four grandparents' family names: Lampe, Holtmeyer, Theising, and Fuchtmann. Yes, you heard that one correctly. Fuchtmann is pronounced with a soft "U" (Fosh-man). In some parts of Germany, it is pronounced differently. I remember listening to Grandma discussing that family name with her two sisters, who giggled. I was just a kid and didn't get the joke then.

Shortly before her death, Rose made a pilgrimage back to Germany to search for her family origins in Germany. I was ten or eleven and amazed she would travel to a foreign country without speaking the language. I think she traveled in Germany by bus from town to town. Her goal was to find any living family and more details about her family tree.

When she returned, I was excited to see what she had learned. I spent frequent weekends at my grandparents' house, so I asked her about her trip on my first weekend upon her return. She told me she was still tired from the journey and might talk to me about it next time. After not learning about the trip on several subsequent visits, I began to think something was wrong. I insisted on seeing the Bible again. Grandma Rose swore me to secrecy before she opened the Bible; I couldn't tell a soul what I was about to see. She had erased one significant branch of the tree, which wasn't easy since it was written in ink. My ten-year-old impetuous self immediately asked, "Grandma, did you make a mistake?" She shushed me, told me about some things she had learned, and added to the family tree, ignoring my interrogation on the erasure. I wasn't listening and kept pestering her about the giant erasure the whole weekend. I can't remember when she finally told me; it might have happened on a subsequent visit; I kept bugging her until she gave it up.

Grandma Rose again swore me to secrecy about the erasure. She got very emotional and broke down crying, telling me she found evidence that this branch had a man who had been hung as a horse thief back in Germany. I then pressed her for details. To a ten-year-old boy, this story was incredible and way more than just ordinary birth and death dates of people I didn't know. She told me this was the last time she would ever speak of this incident. And she kept her word. She was a very proper lady and a horse thief in the family was too traumatic for her to bear.

I was around 14 when she passed away. After my father returned from cleaning out her house to prepare it for sale, I asked him if I could see that old Bible. He said, "I threw that old ratty thing out in the trash" I was shocked beyond belief and furious. The amount of work alone that went into those documents was priceless. Family history just tossed away was inexcusable in my teenage brain. Still today, in my septuagenarian brain, it infuriates me. I swore to myself that one day I would find that horse thief.

In the basement of my grandparents' home were the woodworking tools from Gerhard Lampe, Rose's father. He was a master cabinet maker for one of the furniture manufacturers in Shelbyville. Handmade wood profile planes, rat tail files, scroll saws, brace & bit, chisels, clamps, etc. The tools filled up an entire workbench. I used to play with them, pretending that I was a carpenter. These weren't thrown away but were sold for what I thought was a meager value to clear out the space.

It has always gnawed away at me that Rose's Bible, with all that incredible family history, had been so callously tossed in the rubbish. So, finally, around about forty, I decided to search for Grandma Roses's horse thief. My wife and I got the genealogy bug big time. We took genealogy vacations chasing our family trees and spending time in libraries, courthouses, graveyards, and historical societies. I am proud to say I have documented all four of her grandparents' families back to their arrival in the United

States. They didn't come together but followed similar migration paths in the mid-1800s. They arrived at the Port of New Orleans to settle in Cincinnati. Then they moved to the German Catholic enclave of Oldenburg, Indiana, before finally settling in my hometown, Shelbyville, Indiana. I also found that my grandfather's ancestors were Scottish, not German arriving in the US in Virginia about 1740, and Young was not the original family name. I will say more about that story later.

I have yet to locate that infamous 'horse thief" in Germany, but the search continues. I promise to continue the search with the passion of Richard Kimball, "The Fugitive," who vowed to catch the one-armed man who killed his wife.

A Very Humbling Moment

I was a decent tennis player in high school and continued playing as a young adult. The only problem was that tennis was a seasonal summer sport in Indiana. In the off-season, the only way for me to play was by driving thirty miles and paying steep fees for an indoor tennis club membership. Racquetball was becoming a thing in the 1970s; a club opened in my town at very reasonable rates. So, I started playing racquetball during the off-tennis season.

It turned out racquetball was an effortless transition from my tennis skills; the learning curve was quick. It was also a fun sport, plus I was beginning to need exercise to keep my early dadbod under control. The various clubs in the area started having racquetball tournaments on weekends. These turned into fun getaways, plus you got a free T-shirt. They also offered different levels of competition: Open (professional-cash prizes), A, B, C, and Novice classes. Yes, Professional Racquetball was a real thing. The Indiana State Racquetball Association kept records on everyone's performance in these competitions and ranked the players. I started in the C level and moved up quickly to the B level. I was beginning to get frustrated because my ranking in the B level had plateaued. My competitive drive started having me evaluate the competitors who were beating me. I discovered that most of them were also runners, thus in better shape than me.

So, I started running in addition to tennis and racquetball. My overall fitness level improved tremendously. After about six months, I had worked up to running 10-12 miles a week. My racquetball buddies told me I should start entering some races with them.

Okay, here comes the humbling part of the story. In the

middle of July, I entered a race in Indianapolis. My friends suggested I start by entering the 5K race; as seasoned runners they were doing, they would do the 10K run. If you don't know, like I didn't, a 5K race is 3.1 miles. My daily runs have been close to that distance, so I thought it was within reach. I little stretch, but what the heck, No Pain, No Gain.

The day of the race was a typical sultry Hoosier summer day. The temp was in the 90s, with no clouds in sight, and the humidity was close to 100%. Just walking to the car, you would break a sweat. There was no breeze; you could cut the air with a knife. The race was getting ready to start with about 400 people in this division. I mimicked the other runners leaning on lamp posts and benches, stretching my glutes and hammies. That is what my buddies told me to do; I figured it was a runner thing. The fastest runners lined up in the front. It seemed like it would be fairer in reverse order, but that was the custom. My buddies told me not to take off too fast because the adrenaline kicked in, and I'd have trouble finishing the race. So, I planned to stay within my abilities.

OK, Bang! The starter pistol goes off, and the race starts. The speedy people out front start pulling away. In the back of the pack, we start at a fast walk, and after a few steps, there is room to start jogging. I am starting to get into a rhythm. It is a little faster than I usually run, but it's good to push yourself, right? A half mile into this 3.1-mile run, I look to my right, and a young lady, obviously almost nine months pregnant, pulls up next to me. At this point, I am running faster than my usual speed. As I looked over at her, she looked at me, smiled, and started pulling away. My male reptilian brain kicked in. I thought, "Nope, no pregnant lady is going to beat me." I kicked it into high gear and finally caught up with her halfway through the race. I pull even with her, sweating profusely and breathing like a Bob Baffert racehorse on steroids. Again, I looked over at her; not a sign of labored breathing nor a bead of sweat on her. She glances at me again, laughs aloud this time, and takes off. At this point, I'm dying, thinking, "Shouldn't she be struggling to waddle at this stage of pregnancy, but I can't even keep up with her." Now, the end of the race is in sight, and the last quarter mile is uphill. My reptilian brain again spots her a few people ahead of me. 'OK, last push, I will bury her in this uphill section". I am sprinting as fast as I have ever run in my life. As I passed her, she looked over at me again, kicked on her afterburners or secret pregnancy powers, and easily pulled away from me.

I reached the finish line well after she finished ahead way in front of me. Photographers surround her, snapping photos, while everyone gathers to talk to her. She didn't win the race; we were in the middle of the pack. What the heck is going on?? I walked off the road and fell to my knees in the grass, puking like a dog that ate a spoiled turkey out of the garbage. I was dying, and she wasn't even sweating. The next day, in the newspaper, I saw a photo of her with a story about this Olympian runner out for a light run before she gave birth. I have since forgotten her name, but not the pain. In between hurls, I vowed never to let a pregnant lady beat me again. Yes, you guessed it, I never entered another 5K race again. I keep my vows.

I am so grateful they cropped me out of the photo.

Free Range Religion

Alfred E Neuman and Mad magazine greatly influenced my early religious development. My grandmother frequently dragged me to the Saint Joseph Catholic Church for high mass in Latin. She had difficulty controlling me since I was a very active young tike. Her efforts to educate me about the beliefs and values of her religion were not sinking in. My parents decided it best to send me to Sunday school at the local Presbyterian church, thinking that might be the answer. They teamed up with my buddy, Wilton, from across the street, so we enrolled in their Sunday school program.

Despite the Presbyterians having an excellent big pipe organ and playing rousing songs like Onward, Christian Soldiers. The Christian meaning of that song still escapes me 60 years later, but it was a natural foot stomper. Wilton and I were not great fans of sitting in boring Sunday school learning about the Bible, so we decided to ditch it and have some fun. We were 9 or 10 when we hatched a plot to subvert this attempt at religious indoctrination. I honestly can't remember who the brains behind this plan were. We would get dressed up on Sunday mornings, wearing white shirts, clip-on ties, and sports jackets. As we were ready to head out the door to learn about God and Jesus, we would hit our parents up for the collection plate money for the latest church project.

Here is where reality deviated from our parents' plan. We would walk a few blocks to the church and go in the front door a little early. We would make sure the minister, neighbors, fellow students, and our teachers saw us before we snuck out the back door. We were in and out before anyone was the wiser. Less than a block away was a drugstore with a soda fountain counter and a great magazine rack open early Sunday mornings. It was one of the few establishments open in town. At that time, our town still strictly observed Sunday Blue Laws restricting most commercial activities. This became our oasis away from religious training.

We would buy some magazines and Marvel comics depending on how much money we scammed from our parents that week. We would also treat ourselves to milkshakes or cherry/vanilla fountain sodas. That soda fountain counter is where I grew to love Mad magazine with Alfred E Neuman, Spy vs. Spy stories, and Gahan Wilson and Don Martin cartoons. Alfred had a face that didn't have any care in the world except for mischief. He was my idol. I didn’t always get the jokes, but Wilton and I would still laugh, and act grown up. I also remember reading a Popular Science magazine with a formula for making black powder. That magazine always had interesting ideas for future projects. You never know when a bored middle school student might need the knowledge of how to blow something up. That church pipe organ was pumping out inspirational tunes like ‘Onward, Christian Soldiers.’

Sunday School Soda Fountain

Wilton and I would sit on those round stools readings until it was time to “leave the church.” This was not every Sunday event, but I think you can tell from my weird sense of humor, knowledge of making black powder, and lack of Bible skills that we didn't attend Sunday school very often.

Looking back, I have no idea how Wilton and I didn't get caught. Our parents felt good since we were helping fund missionary projects in some poor countries and learning Bible study skills.

What… me worry?

The First Time I Got My Mouth Washed Out with Soap

The St Mary Street neighborhood was chock full of kids approximately my age. When I was about five years old, I received a gift from my grandparents: a swing set. You know the standard configuration with two swings, a glider, a small metal slide, a trapeze bar, and rings. After my grandfather installed it in our tiny backyard, I enjoyed playing pretend while swinging. I liked pretending I was a pilot while riding as high as possible. My mother enjoyed me playing outside so that I wouldn't wake my baby siblings, so she encouraged me to play on it.

After a while, it got boring playing on this beautiful piece of equipment all by my lonesome. So, I started sharing, inviting other neighborhood kids my age to play. Most of the kids in the neighborhood just had a tree swing, you know, a couple of ropes hung down from a tree limb with a wooden seat or maybe an old car tire. I had the newest kid attraction on the block. Soon the word got out about my glorious new backyard attraction. Three doors down were some older twin boys, Frank and Ralph Jones. As my mom called them, those 'damn Jones twins.' They had a reputation for mayhem in the neighborhood. They never wanted to play with me before the swing set since I was just five-year-old kid two years younger than them. They were too cool to hang out with me until it arrived.

The Jones twins started coming over, asking to play with me. They wanted to use my swing set but knew they had to pretend to play with me. I was thrilled to get attention from the big kids on the block. Reluctantly my mom allowed them to come into the backyard. All my friends my age played nicely on my swing set and didn't get wild. The

Jones boys, however, were crazy wild. They would swing as high as possible; they claimed they would do a loop-de-loop over-the-top bar. I don't think they ever went over the top but would jump off the swing at its apex. That's a word we kindergarteners learned in Mrs. Cooper's class.

The Jones boys were so rambunctious that my very fantastic new swing set was taking a beating. One time they were swinging together in exact unison, being twins. They were always trying to outdo each other, so they kept going higher and higher in precise harmony until the leg posts of the swing set lifted out of the ground tipping the entire unit over. The thing nearly hit me standing since I watched the twins in amazement behind them. My mother heard the loud crash and came running out, thinking someone would be injured, maimed, or dead. The Jones twins skedaddled home faster than the wind, leaving me to try to explain what had happened. The poles attached to the glider to the frame were bent, and it never worked quite the same again. That following weekend my grandpa came over with a sack of concrete and anchored the legs of the swing set deep in the ground. He said that should keep this puppy anchored in the dirt. I kept trying to tell Grandpa George it wasn't my fault.

As the summer went on, Frank and Ralph continued to come over and "play with me." The slide was dented and bent beyond use by them walking up the slide and jumping up and down on it. They got in the glider and rocked it violently back and forth until the hinges at the top broke. Grandpa tried to fix it, but it ended up getting thrown away. Before long, the nice shiny swing set was a dilapidated frame with just the trapeze bar. The twins removed the swing seats; they must have had fingers of steel to twist the screws and nuts off.

My mother finally had it with those twins; too many times, I came into the house crying after the twins got too rough. She banned them from our yard. She would open the back door if they forgot, wander in the yard, and yell, "Go Home, Jones Twins." They were none too happy with my mom. They resented being 86'd from my yard.

So, this is when I got my mouth washed out with soap for the first time. I still interact with them when I road my tricycle out on the sidewalk in front of our houses. My mom couldn't ban them from the sidewalk. These guys were advanced beyond their years and held a grudge like crazy. They taught me new words to call my mom to get back at her. They said she would like it when I called her these words. I looked up to these older boys; they were cool. I trusted what they said and had no reason to believe they would lead me into trouble.

They help me learn and practice these words. This phrase sounded great, even though I didn't know what it meant. They said I had learned the words perfectly, and it was time to go inside and tell them to my mother.
I walked into the house and casually said to my mother, "Hello Fu*^#*ng B*^ch." I was growing up; I had learned some new words and recited them with great aplomb. My pride quickly evaporated as my mom exploded in shock and anger. After she scraped herself off the ceiling, the interrogation began. What did I say? Why did I say it? Who and where did I learn them from? I fessed up right away. I threw the Jones twins under the bus and backed it up a few times. I knew I was in huge trouble. I told her I didn't know what the words meant and that the Jones Twins taught me to say them and encouraged me to ask them. It was like the scene from the Christmas Story movie when Ralphie threw Swartz under the bus when he said the "F" word. My mom was on the phone, immediately yelling at the Jones Twin's

mom. After she hung up, she was back immediately dealing with me. I had to put a soap bar in my mouth and hold it there for a minute. The entire time I had the soap in my mouth, she was yelling at me about how I would never utter those disgusting words again. She also banned me from ever playing with the rotten Jones boys. I learned a valuable lesson that day, never trust the Jones twins. They soon moved across town near my grandparents. I often wondered if they had moved because of that incident. A new family moved in that had two girls my age.

Free Range Pets

As I look back, the pets I had as a kid were also free-range. What else would you expect from a free-range kid? I was always on the hustle to get a pet of some kind.

One of the first pets I remember was a kitten I found on our street. She was pure white, and I called her Snowball. My mom couldn't refuse since I already had a name for her when I brought her in the front door. Mom wasn't fond of cats, but she tolerated my whims. Snowball grew from a tiny, fluffy, cute kitten into a full-sized mean cat that decided she didn't want to be just an indoor cat, so she got to come and go from the house as she pleased. My parents had her fixed. I didn't even know she was broken.

When I was four, I talked my dad into buying me a parakeet and a cage from the Five and Dime store. Casey was mainly green with some yellow and black highlights. His cage was put on the bookshelf behind the sofa in our living room. That made it easy for me to watch him fly around his little cage. I would open the little door and try to touch him. Eventually, I got him to land on my finger. As time went on, Casey got tamer and tamer. I decided he wanted freedom from his tiny cage, so I grabbed him with both hands, pulled him out, and sat on the couch, holding him tightly. When he finally calmed down, I removed my hand so he could perch on my finger. That is when Snowball discovered we had a bird in the house. Fur and Feathers flew, and the chase was on. Oh no! I remember screaming that my cat wanted to eat my bird, but my mother came to the rescue. The cat was put outside, and the bird finally calmed down and landed so we could return him to the cage.

Casey gradually got more and more freedom. He used to sit

on my shoulder, nibbling on my ear while I ate my breakfast. I would give him scraps of my toast to eat. He eventually had free reign of the house, flying from his open cage door as he pleased. At night, he had to stay in the covered cage so he could go to sleep. The cat and the bird never made friends. My mother caught the cat multiple times trying to get into the cage whenever she tossed Snowball out the front door.

One night we were having popcorn while watching TV, and Casey was flying free around the house. I gave him bits of popcorn, and he loved it. I got off the couch, went to the bathroom, and came running back into the living room. I overlooked Casey on the floor, eating some dropped popcorn, and stepped on him. Mighty Casey let out his last chirp. I was heartbroken that not only was Casey dead, but it was also my fault. My parents helped me plan a funeral for my departed buddy. I didn't understand death, but I understood Casey would never fly again.
A shoe box was lined with tissue paper, and a hole was dug in the backyard. The neighborhood kids came, and we said goodbye to Casey. That's what my parents thought. Way before Steven King even thought of his book, Pet Cemetery; I had other plans for Casey. Not understanding death at age four, I exhumed Casey's shoebox and attempted to play with him regularly. I didn't dig him up every day, but my mother saw me one day and was horrified. Casey and the shoebox were moved that evening by my father. I am not sure where, but my guess is the garbage can. Not long after that, Snowball didn't come home. I found her the next day in the street, having been run over by a car. I don't think we had a funeral for Snowball.

Being 0 for 2 in the pet department didn't stop me from my quest. Mom said no more birds or cats. That meant dogs were OK. One of my favorite TV shows was The Adventures of Rin Tin Tin. The lead character was Rusty, a boy orphaned in an Indian raid, whom the soldiers were raising at a U.S. Cavalry post known as Fort Apache. Rusty and his German shepherd dog, Rin Tin Tin, helped the soldiers establish order in the American West. Rin Tin Tin was an intelligent and brave German Shepard who saved the day in each episode. "Yo Rinny" was the cry Rusty would shout out when he wanted Rinny to act against the bad guys. I needed my own Rin Tin Tin to fight the bad guys like Rusty.

My parental units didn't say NO to getting a dog, but they weren't rushing to get me a Rin Tin Tin either. I would have settled for a Lassie. So, I decided to take the issue into my own hands. Since I was allowed to wander on my block, I decided to be on the lookout for stray dogs that needed a good owner.

One day, this great puppy showed up in our neighborhood; I said great because he didn't try to bite me. He looked like he wanted to come home with me, so I grabbed a hunk of rope and tied it around Rin Tin Tin's neck so he could follow me home. I had a dog, and now my job was to convince my mother to keep him. She liked dogs better than cats, so it was not a hard job. A quick survey of the neighborhood convinced her it wasn't a

George, Rin Tin Tin, Kent

lost dog; Rinny was mine. I promised to feed, water, and walk him forever. Rinny was neither a German Shepard nor big and tough, but I had a dog. My mom called him a sooner. He'd sooner pee inside than outside. That was a minor issue, and my mom dealt with it okay.

Rinny and I were best buddies. He slept in my bed, and we were together outside constantly. I kept him on the rope because he would forget and take off. Even though I tried my best to train him to get the bad guys, my "Yo Rinny" shouts didn't inspire him to capture the crooks. He grew into a big ugly dog that chewed on everything in the house and never really learned how to go potty outside. I always kept him on my rope so he wouldn't wander away. One day when I wasn't looking, he wandered off and never came home. I still wonder if Rinny went to live on a farm with other dogs and animals, as my parents said.

I got a pet Chameleon from the Five and Dime store a while later. We got a small aquarium with him to live in. My mom wasn't thrilled I had a lizard, even though he could change his color to blend in with whatever he was sitting on. Freddy had a red piece of yarn tied loosely to his leg that I would attach to my shirt so he could ride around the house with me. I always hoped he would change his skin to a stripe color to match my shirts. That never seemed to work.

I am unsure of the original plan to feed Freddy, but I tried to gather dead flies and other bugs. I'm not sure Freddy liked that too much. I decided he must want to catch his dinner. He had this piece of red yarn on his leg, so you could see that even if he blended into the background of what he was sitting on. In our living room, we had these tall windows with long dark green curtains. I decided it would be best if Freddy went on a hunting expedition to catch his dinner. I put him on the curtain and watched as he climbed around, dragging that piece of yarn, and he changed to dark green. It would be easy to retrieve him when it was time to return to his cage because that red yarn stood out. I went to get Freddy after letting him Free Range for his dinner, I saw the red yarn high up on the curtain, but he was blending into the green curtain.

I couldn't see him. I yelled for Mom to help me find him. This was the first she had heard of this free-range lizard plan. She was not pleased one bit. She grabbed the yarn for me, but Freddy had already slipped out of his leash. Wow, she began using words I'd never heard her say. Of them, I didn't have a clue what they meant. My father came running as she demanded he better find that F&@*ing lizard. I wasn't worried; how hard would it be to find a tiny chameleon on a tall green curtain? Sadly, Freddy never came back. Maybe he went to live on the farm with Rinny?

I decided it was best to cool it on the pet thing for a while since it hadn't gone so swell so far. It was close to Halloween, and my buddy Darryl and I got some dry corn ears to prepare for Trick or Treat. We meant it back in those days- No Treat meant you got a Trick. We weren't like some awful kids; we didn't soap people's windows and screens. We would merely throw handfuls of shelled corn kernels, making a horrible racket and a mess to lean up if we didn't get a treat.

In my bedroom, where I was storing these ears of corn, was a window that looked out over a roof on the second floor. One day I noticed a beautiful pigeon strutting and cooing on the roof outside my window. This pigeon was not the standard grey color but a beautiful multicolored beige and light brown color. I wondered what they ate, so I grabbed a few kernels of corn, slowly opened the window a crack, and tossed them to him. He ate the corn and took off. Wow, that was cool. I had previously attempted to capture pigeons with a cardboard box propped up with a string attached to a stick, waiting for the bird to wander under the box. That was a wasted afternoon. But I had gotten a pigeon within a few feet of my bedroom window. Cool.

The next day, I looked out the window, and the pigeon was back. I cracked the window and tossed a few more pieces of corn. Cool, I had a secret pet that I named Waldo. A few days later, Waldo showed up with a couple of buddies. Wow, I was a real pigeon wrangler. I kept feeding my growing flock. The area right below my window was our front porch. My parents were starting to complain about the pigeon poop that was showing up on only our front stoop. I couldn't imagine Waldo and friends making my parents hose off the steps so often. They started sleeping outside my window, and I could hear them cooing when I went to sleep and upon waking.

One day, my mom noticed a mess of corn debris in my room while cleaning. I confessed to her Darryl and my plan for Halloween tricks. She saw my window slightly cracked open and went to shut it when she saw all the corn debris and pigeon feathers outside on the roof. Busted, I confessed to having Waldo as a secret pet, and he brought his buddies to visit. My Halloween trick plan was a failure, and my personal pet pigeon flock was nixed. It took a couple of weeks of not feeding the birds to abate the stoop poop problem.

Our little town had many pigeons that lived in the downtown area. I occasionally saw Waldo among the flock when riding my bike around the town square. He was easy to spot because of his light coloring among all the darker-colored birds. The city council decided the pigeons had become a health concern and organized a plan to cull the flock. Men were stationed on rooftops with shotguns with instructions to shoot as many birds as possible. The birds would fly away from their roost only to return to more blasts. I never saw Waldo again and wondered if he survived that day to go live on the farm with Rinny and Freddy.

Many dogs followed me home over my childhood and even a few times as an adult. One of the best dogs that joined our family just showed up on our porch one cold winter evening. I heard a small dog whimpering and scratching our door to get in. My parents said it was probably someone's pet and would find its way home. They told me to leave it alone. It was such a bitterly cold and snowy night. I kept checking, and it was still there half dead. I finally begged them enough that we let the poor thing in. It turns out it was a little brown Pomeranian, hardly weighing 4 pounds. I promised to look for Sparky's owners the next day. Yes, I already had a name for the little guy. My parents knew we had another pet. I put an ad in the newspaper lost and found section and went door to door in the neighborhood, unsuccessfully trying to find his home. He was an adult dog and already house-trained. Sparky was a natural, free-range dog that separated from his family and found us. He lived the rest of his life with us. He was no Rin Tin Tin but a good dog nonetheless.

The last pet I will tell you about, I am not even sure if it qualifies as a pet, was an Easter chick. The Five and Dime sold hundreds of these baby chicks at Easter time that were dyed blue, pink, and orange to kids, only to die horrible deaths soon after Easter. Mine survived that early death sentence and grew into a gangly teenage chicken. When we first got Henny Penny, it made cute little cheep cheep noises and lived in a cardboard box in our downstairs bathroom. Henny had lost her downy feathers and was now getting real chicken feathers and making lots of noise. My parents discussed taking Henny Penny to the farm to see Rinny, Freddy, and Waldo. Henny Penny wasn't a great pet, it couldn't fetch a stick or a ball, so I wasn't that interested in her. My parents had a party one evening, and everyone had many adult beverages when one of the party-goers went to use the toilet. Henny Penny got startled and started flying around the room, hit her head on the wall, fell into the toilet, and drowned. The guest was very disturbed that he had killed my chicken. I told him it was okay; at least he didn't have to go to live on the farm.

School Disruptor

My entire public-school career was a bland, non-descript series of events. I was never the teachers' focus since I was neither a failing nor a star student; I was firmly planted in the middle of the bell curve. I don't believe I ever volunteered to the teachers' calls to their questions, but I would always answer when called upon. Likewise, my behavior goal was to never get into trouble. I'll bet that if you surveyed all my former teachers, very few would even remember me.

My attitude toward school behavior changed my senior year when they hired a new physics teacher. I will call him Teacher "L." In this story, "L" was not just an ineffective teacher; he was totally clueless about the subject matter he was teaching. "L" had previously only taught remedial math; at least, that's what I recall. I also doubt he ever taught science before. It seemed he may have never taken a class in physics. Starting day one, this teacher had zero credibility and immediately lost control of his classes. In short, "L" was the worst teacher I ever had.

The physics classroom had large lab table desks with two students per desk so we could have labs and experiments, which we never did. The classroom wasn't full, so several of the desks were unused. I wasn't involved in this bit of classroom sabotage but followed the progress daily. "L" would sit on the

Lab Desk

unoccupied desk rather than stand in front of the class while teaching. Before school started each day, students would use screwdrivers and wrenches to slowly loosen the hardware in the unused desk. Bit by bit, the knobs, drawer pulls, entire drawers, and doors were removed from the classroom one at a time. After several weeks the desk was just a mere skeleton held together with a couple of bolts, and you might say a wing and a prayer. "L" was clueless and continued to sit on it, unaware of impending doom. The day arrived when all the structural bolts were removed, and it was just stacked pieces of wood like a giant Jenga game waiting to tumble. "L" began his lesson and leaned on the table, causing the whole structure to collapse onto the floor. Total classroom chaos erupted; "L" wasn't injured, but word of this prank quickly spread throughout the entire school. Despite the ensuing investigation, no one was ever disciplined since no one could be identified. This is how school legends were made.

Before this, "L" had already lost control of his classroom; neighboring teachers would pop into his room to help lower the noise. Since "L" didn't have a clue about the subject matter he was supposed to teach, students would often challenge the lessons he was trying to convey. We had a transfer student, Bob, from another school who had already taken an advanced physics class at his other school the year prior. Bob was a brilliant student who later graduated from Purdue with a triple major in Physics, Math, and Chemistry. Often, he would find fault with "L" teaching and argue with him until he won. It went beyond arguing actual knowledge; we egged Bob to make up BS to mess with "L." The most famous instance of this came when we were studying light. That day, Bob asked "L" about this universal physical constant. He postulated that if you had the speed of "Light "traveling from the left at 186,000 miles per second in a vacuum and you had the speed of "Dark" traveling from the right at 186,000 miles per second in a vacuum. What would happen at the intersection of these two constants? Bob added that we know there must be a speed of dark because of Newton's third law of physics that force is an interaction between objects, and forces exist in equal-and-opposite pairs. "L" was at a total loss to explain what would occur at the intersection of such immense forces. Bob then dropped the bomb; the Speed of Dim would be at the intersection of the Speed of Light and Dark. The class erupted into laughter. "L" was left stammering, unable to counter this total BS theory. Carpe Diem. The torture didn't end there.

"L" had a bad verbalization hesitation habit that progressively worsened as the school year continued. He would use the word "Uhhh" as a sentence filler. I don't just mean occasionally but almost constantly. One day in class, I was bored and counted him saying "Uhhhh" 70 times. I am sure that since everything he said was critiqued, he constantly had to rethink what he was getting ready to say. It doesn't matter why, but it was getting so bad. Academics call them disfluencies — that diminish credibility and distract from the message. We, kids, would all talk about "L's" bad habit and wonder how many times a day he said it.

"L" cartoon by Darryl

His classroom had a small office where a phone was located. One day the phone rang, and he left the room to answer the phone, mid-sentence saying "Uhhhhh," and two minutes later, he reentered the classroom saying "Uhhhhh," thus establishing the longest "Uhhhh" on record.

This was the only time I became a disruptor in my school career. I organized a lottery to guess how many times "L" would say "Uhhhh" a day. The plan was that we all would put a quarter into the pot to go to the winner who guessed the correct number. I got people to sign up to be "official" counters in each of his classes and eventually signed up backup counters to ensure we got an accurate count. The contest was on; we selected a date for the great "Uhhhh Count-Off." What great fun this would be!

The "Uhhh Count Off" day arrived, and the whole school was abuzz. The first-class period went off with no issues, the official counters agreed their counts were correct and stood at 43. The following two classes also went as planned; it was the 4th-period class where things unraveled. "L" started noticing people watching the counters record each "Uhhh." He began to wonder aloud and said "Uhhhh" and saw the counters making a tally mark on their notebooks which caused him to say "Uhhhh" again which got another tally mark. The jig was up, he exploded, and the administration got involved and shut down our Lottery. My counters ratted me out as the instigator, planner, and bookie. I got called to the principal's office for the first time in my school career.

The principal was very upset with me when I arrived at his office. I confessed to everything and was expecting to get expelled or, maybe worse- a note on my 'permanent record'. The principal had my student record card out, remarking that I had zero discipline notes in my file. He finally calmed down enough that I could explain what a poor excuse of a physics teacher he was. I was surprised when he agreed with me and actually said it was their fault for not being able to recruit a good teacher for us students.

Wow, what a turn of events; I didn't see that coming. He said that it would be impossible to find a replacement teacher mid-year and asked me to ease up on the harassment. He didn't say stop; ease up. My punishment was to sit in his outer office until the period was over and then return to my regular class schedule. The next day went off like the Great "Uhhh" Count Off had never happened. I think I had to refund the quarters to those who paid. The following year they replaced "L" with a qualified physics teacher. Of course, I was off to college and never benefited from the improved science instruction.

Two Prom Dates

Despite being very new to the dating scene, I had two dates to the Prom during my junior year in high school. You might remember my story about efforts to secure a date to Simon and Garfunkel in April 1967. Yes, I went from being a gangly gawky nerd without any dates to having two in one evening for our Jr. Sr. Prom in May. The only thing I can attribute to my becoming a babe magnet was being one of the stars of our tennis team. Yes, high school tennis players were hunks of masculinity.

In 1967, my Junior year, I was one of the veteran players on our tennis team. Back then, we played two seasons of tennis, fall and spring. We didn't stop playing during the winter; we didn't have any tennis meets. Indoor tennis courts were a rarity back then. However, we had access to the girls' basketball gym at the junior high school with a brick wall to practice hitting our forehand and backhand shots. We marked the wall with tape at 36 inches to simulate the net height in the middle of the court. We would hit the tennis ball against the wall and then get ready for the ball to rebound back at us and hit it back. We had different drills, all forehand, all backhand, or alternating both sides. The wall being brick meant it was constantly bouncing a little differently than a perfectly flat wall. You had to be on your toes literally to keep the ball moving. In addition to this ball drill, we would work on our aerobic conditioning by playing basketball games. The girls' gym hoop was lowered to 9 feet from the standard 10 feet in the boys' gym. Being Hoosiers, every one of us tennis boys wished we could have been on the basketball team. Playing on this court allowed us to fulfill our dreams by being able almost to dunk the basketball. I think I touched the regulation rim once.

The tennis team was a tight-knit group since most of us started together as freshmen. Our first year's record was pathetic, followed by good improvement in our sophomore year. During the summers, we played a lot of tennis at the city parks in the evenings among ourselves and any adults who showed up. Our game was improving and our tennis also. Ha.

Girls would come down to the park to play tennis during the summer. We only had two courts, so we had lots of downtime to socialize while waiting for a court to open up. Depending on the size of the crowd waiting, one set was usually the limit. The parks department had installed lights and built some lovely benches, which became our gathering spot.

In 1967, my junior year, most of our team were all juniors except for our star player, Jack, a grade younger. He was always our Ace player and would always take on our high school opponents' #1 player. Jack started going steady with Diane, one of the girls who came to the courts to watch the tennis action. She was a junior, like most of the team. We all tended to socialize as a group. During my junior year, our fall season started, and our team was developing into a powerhouse. We won almost all our matches. Things were going very well. Diane began to talk about the Jr-Sr Prom that was coming spring. I thought it odd since her boyfriend, Jack, our Ace player, was a sophomore and would not be able to attend. Not understanding the feminine mind back then, I ignored her, always rambling about the Prom. I noticed that when our little clique gathered together and if Jack left, Diane would start saying things like, "Gee, I wish I could go to the Prom." I am thinking, geez, this event is six months in the future. Little did I know that girls planned and dreamed about these events all their lives. I had not even had a date, let alone thought about a formal dance. Just thinking about that made me sweat. Diane was relentless; whenever Jack wasn't around, it seemed all she talked about in the halls or cafeteria was the Prom.

One day when Diane and I were waiting for class to start, she blurted out, "Gee Whiz, I sure wish someone would ask me to the Prom!" I asked if she had broken up with Jack, and she replied that she had not and said Jack wouldn't mind if someone else took her to Prom since he couldn't attend. I'm unsure what I said, but I thought that was odd. Why is she telling me this?

I didn't have any romantic feelings for Diane; she was one of the gang and Jack's girl. I started feeling sorry for her not being able to go to Prom. Slowly, my idiot adolescent male brain was beginning to realize she wanted me to ask her to Prom. All these Prom conversations were not just idle conversations but hints aimed directly at me. Ack, what should I do? If I ask her out, will that wreck the tennis team 'esprit de corps'?

So, I finally told Diane I didn't know how to dance, hoping that would end the conversation. The opposite occurred; she said "we" wouldn't have to dance a lot, maybe once or twice. I told her I was uncomfortable taking her to the Prom since she was Jack's girl. I didn't want him to become jealous. She said Jack wouldn't mind and thanked me for asking her to go to the prom. What? I didn't ask her out! I think I was hoodwinked. Jack appeared out of nowhere, and Diane told him I had agreed to take her to the Prom. What the heck just happened?

So, it's December, and the event is six months away. Diane started telling me about her dress and that I should investigate renting a tuxedo and corsage. Suddenly, being a nice guy will cost me some serious money. Meanwhile, Jack is acting very distant despite Diane's statement about how I could make him jealous. That was good for my self-esteem.

Fast forward to April, and I have gotten an actual date to Simon and Garfunkle with Cathy. That date went well, and I started hanging out with her more and more. You might say we were going steady. The Prom was only a month away, and I realized I had best tell her I already had a date to the Prom arranged months and months before our first date. I couldn't possibly back out on Diane at this late date since she had her Prom outfit bought months ago.

Gosh, this dating stuff is so complicated. So, I finally told Cathy that I would like to take her to the Prom, BUT I had previously made this commitment to Diane. Cathy said she understood, but this didn't go over well. I needed to find a way to smooth this over and keep everyone happy.

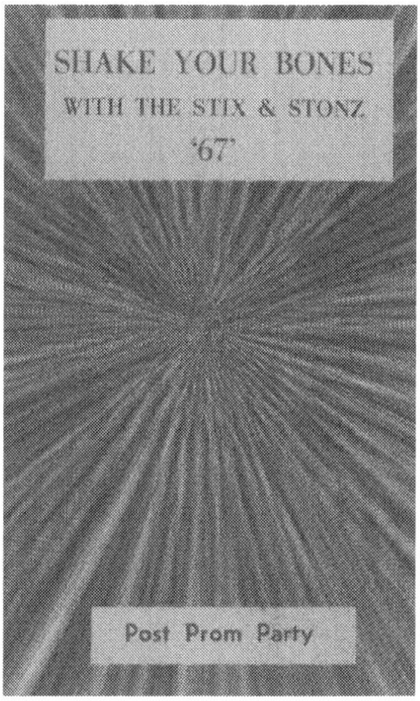

I finally developed a possible solution to my dilemma. A parent group had been doing a post-prom party for several years to keep kids from doing dumb and dangerous stuff after the prom. They rented the local Elks Club and provided entertainment and food for an all-night post-prom party. Once you entered the building, you couldn't leave until after they served breakfast at 7 AM. I talked to Diane and explained the situation. I wanted to get out of my commitment to the Post Prom. To my surprise, she said she hadn't even considered attending that with me.

Now I tell Cathy I want to take her to the Post Prom. I knew this wasn't a traditional arrangement, but it was the best I could do. I planned to rush Diane home after the prom, go to my house to change my tux into a less formal sportscoat, and pick Cathy up in time to get into the Post Prom. They didn't want kids running around after prom, so they closed the doors for entry reasonably soon after the Prom ended and opened them after breakfast. The schedule was doable. Cathy's mother wasn't as amenable to the plan. I think she felt her daughter was being played as a second fiddle. Cathy agreed to be my date for the Post Prom. I even got her a corsage.

I don't remember anything about the Prom; I hope Diane enjoyed it. The Post Prom was a great time. The main act was the Styx and Stonz, a garage band from our town that was getting popular and was now touring nationally: an old vaudeville style comedian, a banjo player, and two balloon artists plus a talent show. We got to stay out all night, plus we had tons of food all evening with breakfast before we went home to sleep.

I went from not having a date to being the only boy to having two dates to the Prom.

Postscript to the story, I began doing my family genealogy in my fifties. One of the dangers of living in a small rural town is that everyone is related to each other. I discovered that Diane is my 4th cousin. So now I can brag that I had two dates to the prom, and I married one of my dates who wasn't my cousin.

Selective Service and Gout

In 1968, all males turning 18 had to register with the Selective Service System after high school. I remember going to see our local Selective Service agent, a very dour-looking lady with the initials "F.M." The Shelby County SSS office was in a small dark room full of file cabinets located in the basement of the post office. I gave "F.M." the information needed to issue my Draft Registration Card (SSS Form 1) that, included: name, Selective Service registration number, age, date and place of birth, ethnicity, place of residence at the time of registration, and basic physical description. I distinctly remember her slamming the typewriter keys harder when I informed her of my student deferment status. I should have realized this foreshadowed my gout affliction years later.

Let me say that I sincerely appreciate the sacrifices made by anyone who has served in our military. However, I felt our involvement in Vietnam in the 1960s was unjustified, and I was firmly against the war even in high school. I continue to think that all the wars we have been involved in since Vietnam have been illegitimate, resulting in millions of people needlessly dying and suffering. They also have resulted in the most debt racked up by our country since they were never paid for.

Draft Lottery

In my first semester at Indiana University, the first draft lottery since 1942 was held on Dec 1, 1969. This drawing determined the induction order for men born between January 1, 1944, and

December 31, 1950. My July 12th birthday earned me the #15 spot on the list, meaning I would be called up as soon as I graduated or left college. Ironically, the guy across the hall who was gung-ho and ready to serve got #350. We both were very distressed and troubled about the fate of this drawing.

I was not a very studious kid in high school. You might even say I never studied. My study skills could have improved, but I got decent to unexceptional grades through the magic of osmosis by carrying home my books every night with the most excellent intentions. The teachers always told my parents I needed to work to my potential. I guess that means I learned a few things despite myself.

Enrolling in college changed my draft status from I-A (Available for military service) to I-S (Student deferred by statute). This drawing immediately made my need to stay in school crystal clear. This lottery was held almost at the end of the semester, just a few weeks before finals. I started burning the midnight oil to catch up from all the slacking off I had done since I registered in September. I could barely salvage the semester, but it ignited a renewed vigor to study. My grades improved every semester after that as I honed my studying skills. If I was classified 1-S (student deferment), there was hope that the war would end before I graduated.

I knew I should rely on something other than studying to keep me from losing my deferment. The anti-war movement was growing at Indiana University like it was nationwide, so I sought other options. I found a group that provided draft counseling. I was adamant that I wouldn't do anything illegal, like moving to Canada to evade the draft, but I wanted to explore all legal options to avoid going to Vietnam. Always a little superstitious, I held onto my draft card until my forties when it died a natural death of too many cycles through the washer. One option this group suggested was to explore a medical deferment. I was a healthy young man, but they insisted it might be possible to find some hidden ailments.

I found a sympathetic doctor who performed a routine physical with X-rays and a full panel of blood tests. The results were promising. I was a healthy 20-year-old male with a slightly elevated uric acid level. Armed with this news, I returned to my draft counselors, who enlisted some pre-meds students to help explore the possibilities. We went to the IU med school library and researched what elevated uric acid levels meant. We discovered that low uric acid levels had no ill effects, but high levels caused several issues. When uric acid reaches a certain level, the body starts secreting crystals into joints, toes, knees, and elbows, causing severe pain. A plan was hatched.

We found out what caused increased uric acid levels; the chief culprit was dietary. Certain foods like red meat, seafood, and port wine would increase uric acid levels. The plan was for me to binge on these foods for a couple of weeks and then go to the student health center with a complaint of knee pain and a history of elevated uric acid. I bought port wine by the half gallon and went to a cheap local steak house every night. The doctor at the health center confirmed that my uric acid levels were elevated—the first record for an appeal for a medical deferment.

I repeated this binging cycle several times with the same results. Boy, that cheap port wine is nasty-tasting stuff. I can't even stand smelling it to this day. My draft counselors helped me draft my appeal for medical deferment, which I sent to my dear friend "F.M." at my local SSS office. She replied that I would need to report for a pre-induction physical at the crack of dawn at her office to take the bus to the Indianapolis Induction Center. I arrived at the prescribed hour with the folder of my evidence. We arrived at the center after several stops at other small towns picking up other young men. The movie Alice's Restaurant was an amazingly accurate depiction of this process.

It turns out I wasn't just presenting my evidence and getting a ruling; I got to experience the entire physical process. We stripped down to shorts and socks and began following orders shouted by sergeants to follow lines of various colors on the floor to various stations for different examinations to be performed. At one station, we supplied urine samples with instructions that we qualified unless we dissolved the swizzle stick. At the next station, they counted our eyes, and if we had two, good enough. You get the drift; nobody failed. The process was focused on making young men eligible to ship overseas.

At the end of the exam came the part where we could appeal special conditions. Like Alice's restaurant, "Kid, I want you to go and sit down on that bench that says Group W, now, kid!" I was instructed to follow a particular color line on the floor and wait on a bench for the Doctor. The young man in front of me had extremely gnarled, arthritic hands. The doctor asked him to demonstrate squeezing a rifle trigger which he did with much pain. "Ok, son, you will be a great soldier" My heart sank; I felt stupid with my achy knee uric acid story. Sure enough, I passed with flying colors.

So, my draft counselors suggested the next step was an appeal of the ruling. The proper forms were submitted, and soon I received notice to report again for another physical at the induction center. I knew the location and decided to skip the trip to my hometown to ride the olive-drab bus to

Indianapolis, thus saving myself several hours. I went through the same Alice's Restaurant process and got to the end with a special note on my file about my appeal. This time the doctor spent a few minutes reading my file and decided maybe the military should take their blood sample to verify my uric acid level. Good thing I had been following my Port wine, high red meat, and seafood diet before this.

OK, now, while waiting for the blood test result. I received notice that my dear friend "F.M." had reported me AWOL since I missed the bus from her office. She indeed turned up the heat on this induction battle. My paperwork showed I had certainly been there and completed the physical. My Selective Service record file was getting thicker.

The government blood test results showed elevated uric acid levels, but they still ruled me as fit for service. I filed another written appeal and was granted an in-person review. This didn't go well; this higher-ranked military person must have smelled a rat. He suggested I report to the barracks for a two-week stay and then have a re-test of my blood. I declined, telling them I couldn't possibly miss two weeks of classwork because I was a serious student. Dang! My file is continuing to swell.

In the following months, I began to explore my options to legally avoid going to Vietnam in what I felt and still believe was an unjust war. I investigated becoming an Australian citizen after I graduated. At that time, they were recruiting people with degrees to come down under and be granted immediate Australian citizenship making me legally exempt from the US Draft.

I investigated joining the Indiana National Guard since they had not been deployed to Vietnam, but openings were nonexistent. Dan Quail, future Mr. 'Potatoe' Head VP, got the last spot, which was my joke.

My draft counselors suggested one last shady trick, I wouldn't say I liked the idea, but I felt the pressure. The plan was to request a copy of my file from my dearest Selective Service official, "F.M."; if she refused, I was to ask her to sign a form stating she had indeed refused my request, which would start a whole process for another appeal. So, I went to my hometown, entered her office, and asked for a copy of my file. "F.M." had steam coming out her ears; she told me she didn't have a copy machine and would have to type certified copies of my thick file. I said that I would be glad to wait. I sat in the corner while she pounded on her government-issued olive drab Underwood typewriter. At one point, I almost told her to stop because I had no legitimate use for my file, but I suddenly remembered she had recently reported me AWOL. I thanked her for the file and returned to the university to continue my studies.

As the clock kept ticking forward on my 4-year student deferment, it was looking more and more inevitable that upon graduation day, "F.M." would be standing on stage to hand me induction papers simultaneously with my diploma. The Vietnam War in 1972 showed no signs of stopping, and the draft machine needed more bodies. I saw no escape from the draft. I usually should have graduated in May 1972, thus immediately triggering the process of my reporting for induction—one last-minute stall tactic I had left to play. I asked two sympathetic professors to give me incompletes, leaving me short credits needed to receive my degree. I reminded "F.M." that I had a 4-year student deferment, not a three-year and 9-month deferment. Yes, that was a bit picky, but I still hoped for some miracle. I had just gotten married the past January, and this whole

military thing was now far more complicated. Yet, another form for my ever-expanding Selective Service file.
I was adamant I would not carry a gun in this unjust war, but I wouldn't break any laws like escaping to Canada. During the summer, I found a medic unit in the Indiana National Guard, which was deploying, that said they would let me sign up. I had planned that by the time I got professionally trained, the war would be winding down, and I wouldn't be needed. So, the clock was ticking to zero on my student deferment. I informed "F.M." of my choice. She told me I must report to the Induction Center to be processed. I vigorously complained; I have been there at least four times already.

I reported one last time to the Induction Center in Indianapolis and started following the colored lines to the various stations from memory. Again, I reached the end where a doctor would declare my fitness for induction into the US Military service as a Medic in the US Army. I felt like I would toss my cookies when it was my turn. The doctor grabbed my very thick file and asked quizzically, "You want to enlist in the Army Medics?" I replied, "Yes, Sir." Then without even opening my file, he grabbed his rubber stamp**. IV-F** and said, "Son, your medical file indicates you have some serious medical issues." He deemed me "not qualified for any military service." There I stood in my jockey shorts and socks, stunned.

Fast forward to my golden years, I now suffer from occasional gout without gorging on port wine, red meat, and seafood. The truth is that gout is no joke, but neither is war. I fully support our young people who serve. I only wish the politicians who sent them into harm's way were less like F.M. and some of the bureaucrats I met at the induction center. I wonder how my dear friend "F.M." got the news of my last physical.

College Rejection

I was heading into my senior year of high school, knowing it was time to think about my future. My parents and school counselors had been yammering about it for quite a while. The Vietnam War was in serious escalation mode, with battles raging on Walter Cronkite's show every night. The government was talking about instituting a draft for military service. This gave me a sudden impetus to go to college and get a student deferment. Throughout high school, I took college preparatory classes. Easy Peasy, I had it all under control. Now, what do I do?

I tried remembering everything my counselors had been yapping about the last several years. Tests, Applications, Campus visits, GPA. Yikes. The lightbulb in my head had finally turned on but immediately burst into flames. I knew I was in trouble, but just not how deep. I made an appointment with my guidance counselor to get help. Mr. Clay smiled and asked, "What brings you in today, George?" With a bit of panic, I said, "I need to go to college." Very calmly, he nodded and said, "Yes, we have been discussing that goal with you for some time. What profession do you want as your future?" "Huh? I just want to go to college."

He explained that each college had different specialties, preparing students for careers. He suggested I take a test that would help me focus on my aptitudes. The following day, he gave me an appointment to take an aptitude test to measure my natural, inborn abilities. This was exciting. Would I be a doctor, lawyer, or maybe a scientist? I took the test and returned the following day excited to learn about my future. Mr. Clay told me my test results were a little ambiguous but that it showed I would be best suited to be a 'Forest Ranger.' Remember that I was born and raised in Indiana, where forests don't exist. This was flat farm country. I think I just stared at him as my bubble burst and my distinguished legal, medical, and scientific careers disappeared.

After a long silence, I asked Mr. Clay, "Does it give a second choice?" Ever the diplomat, he explained these tests are not always accurate and that not everyone has a firm career path established in high school. He went on to say that many people changed their majors in college.
He suggested the best thing for me to do would be to start visiting some college campuses and filling out college applications ASAP. We talked about the upcoming ACT and SATs and how important they would be for college admission since my GPA was not in the upper echelons of my class. As I left for my next class, I wondered what a forest ranger did besides chase bears away from picnic baskets.

I had been a decent tennis player and was a little shocked when I got a recruiting letter from Kalamazoo College. Wow, I was thrilled beyond imagination since I had not even dreamed of playing on the collegiate level. The coach's letter described their tennis program starting their tennis season in January with a three-week tour of the southern states before returning to campus, where they had a six-court indoor facility to play before the weather permitted outdoor play. They hosted the Junior Davis Cup championship every year. I was hooked; where do I sign up? I was going to tour the southern states playing tennis. The coach also included a brochure about the college, but that wasn't important. I doubted they had a forestry program. After I quit bouncing off the walls, I glanced at the school brochure. Founded in 1833, Kalamazoo College was a premier liberal arts institution and one of the nation's 100 oldest colleges and universities. They only had 1,200 students then, which was not much bigger than my high school. Some of the prominent universities I had investigated scared me with so many students.

The academic program they offered was also unique. The K-Plan comprised three core components: career service, foreign study, and the Senior Independent Project (SIP). To accommodate the K-Plan, the College operated on a quarter system. Students would spend their first year on campus taking courses and then spend their sophomore spring off-campus at an internship before going abroad the fall and winter of their junior year. Then, in senior year, they would work independently on their SIPs, a senior thesis of their choosing. Since I had four years of Spanish, the junior year foreign travel was very intriguing.

Kalamazoo College, besides the intriguing tennis opportunity and intriguing academic program, a third exciting element was its proximity to Michigan State, located in Lansing, only 75 miles away. My steady high school girlfriend had a scholarship offer to attend there. The coach's letter included information on an upcoming weekend campus visitation program. I convinced my parents this was my golden opportunity. I filled out the registration for the campus visit and submitted my enrollment application, including my transcript and test scores. When the appointed weekend arrived, we drove up to Kalamazoo, Michigan. Upon arrival, I immediately noticed the campus was beautiful. I attended several campus tours and fell in love with the entire program.
It was time to meet the tennis coach. He gave me a quick tour of the tennis facility and sat me down for a private talk. I thought, OK, here is where I get the information on how much of an athletic scholarship he would offer me. He said, "OK, kid, here's the deal. Your name popped up on my radar because you beat my number 1 player last

summer in that tournament at Ball State. I'd love to have you play for us, but the admissions department has informed me your GPA doesn't meet our admissions standards." I said, "My SAT and ACT scores were much better, and I am doing much better this final semester." He explained that he had no power over the admissions policy. This was an academic institution.

Long story short, I got admitted to Indiana University, where I played intermural tennis. In hindsight, I should have listened to my parents and counselors and applied myself more in high school. Ironically, in 1985, I relocated to Washington State, known for its sprawling mountains and dense forests. After settling into our new home, I started doing lots of hiking. I discovered solace and respite amidst the serene woods, finding peace on weekends away from the bustle of the business world. Reflecting on Mr. Clay's career test, I can't help but wonder if perhaps my true calling was meant to be that of a Forest Ranger.

Gleanings

As I was gathering the stories you have just read, other short memories bubbled to the top of my brain. Nothing of major significance but I decided to record them for posterity.

Petroliana

When I turned 16, I learned how to drive a stick shift dual-wheel stake bed truck with a lift gate. My father said it was time to clean out the old warehouse. My grandfather started Young Oil in 1935 primarily having gasoline filling stations. His generation came through the Depression era and never threw anything away. The warehouse was full of old stuff and junk is the best way I could put it. I grabbed a pair of gloves and loaded the truck full of trash and junk. Now it was time to head to the dump driving a large truck with a stick shift for the first time. It had been raining so the dump was a muddy mess, the dump manager directed me to a spot to unload my load. After slipping and sliding to the spot, I threw all the stuff off the truck into a nice pile and now it was time to head back. The dual wheels of the truck were spinning and digging deep into the mud. Yep, I was stuck. The dump manager saw my dilemma and came to the rescue. He put some boards under the tires and gave me instructions on how to drive in the mud. I now was fully competent to handle a dump run.

I headed back to the warehouse and reported my task was completed. My father walked out and told me I was not even close to being done. He pointed to all the old signs, oil bottles, pumps, globes, racks, etc. If you ever watch the American Pickers TV show, they call this stuff Petroliana Collectables. I was shocked, thinking this stuff was so cool. This was 1966 more than forty years before American

Pickers showed America how collectable this stuff has become. I pleaded to keep some of the best stuff, but I was told to clear the warehouse out of all this old junk. OK, I was making a whopping $1.25 an hour so I didn't object too long. In retrospect, I should have absolutely said "NO F**king Way". At the very least, I should have found a way to hide some of it somewhere.

I didn't remember how many times I loaded that stake truck. Those tall visible pumps had a clear glass cylinder on top and were about nine feet tall. The clear cylinder allowed the customer to see exactly what amount they were getting. The customer could also see the quality of the gas and if it was dirty. I threw out many wire racks with glass bottles holding engine oil. Before disposable metal, paper, and plastic engine oil containers became commonplace, drivers pulling into gas stations and asking for oil often had to watch and wait as the lubricant was hand-pumped from a drum into a glass bottle with a metal spout.

My grandfather changed the brands of oil companies he was distributing several times over the years, so there were multiple brands of signage. Phillips 66, Pure Oil, and Union 76 were some of the brands I remember. The later generation of gas pumps didn't have the glass cylinder to see the gasoline, but they had advertising glass globes on top of the pump that lit up at night. Those pumps and globes were loaded onto the truck and headed for the dump as well.

I took all this history and unceremoniously just threw it all into the garbage pile with the sickening sounds of glass breaking. I didn't think of the monetary value; the sentimental value was staggering. Today all that equipment would have been a small fortune to the collectors. I cleaned out the warehouse and it was spotless and empty. It was then and even more today a dark hole in my soul. My objections were not strong enough. It is weird how some people value the past and others cannot wait to forget it.

Voter registration

When I was eligible to vote at age 21, my fiancé and I went to the courthouse to register to vote in the 1972 election. An elderly gentleman, who I assumed to be a volunteer, said he could get us registered. In the late 1960s, I became very active in politics and was excited to finally vote. He took my soon-to-be wife first; he recognized her name since her mother was an elected official whose office was one floor below. He said he knew my future mother-in-law and a long conversation ensued. When he got done talking and filled out the paperwork, my fiancé was an officially registered Republican voter. In Indiana, you had to register a party if you wanted to vote in the primary.

It was now my turn. He asked my name. When I told him, George E Young, he stopped in his tracks and asked if I was related to George Young, the former postmaster. I replied that he, indeed, was my grandfather. He grabbed my hand and shook it vigorously saying he had worked for my grandfather at the post office and had been great friends ever since. He introduced himself as Louie Neu and couldn't stop gushing about what a great man my grandfather was. I greatly enjoyed meeting a friend of my grandfather and hearing stories from 40 years prior, but it was time to get me registered. He filled in all my personal details and asked for party affiliation. When I said Democrat, I thought he was going to have a heart attack. It was like a scene with Fred Sanford on Sanford and Son. This gentleman said, "NO, no, no, you can't register as a Democrat; your grandfather will roll over in his grave". I repeated that I wanted to be registered as a Democrat. He said he wouldn't do it. Louie suddenly remembered my fiancé's mother; a staunch Republican was just one floor below. He took off almost running, I could hear his footsteps racing down the marble steps to enlist my future mother-in-law's help in preventing this tragedy. He returned in a few minutes scowling put down my form on the counter and turned his back saying someone else would have to complete my registration. He couldn't bring himself to register the grandson of his old buddy as a Democrat.

After the fall election results were announced, I was able to see my vote for Governor for Finley Campbell - Peace and Freedom Party. I cast the only vote for the professor from Wabash College in my entire county of 45,000 people. Finley came in fourth statewide with 6278 votes. I think my grandfather would have been proud because I voted my conscience. I didn't like either of the Democrat or Republican candidates.

Fundraising

Collecting pop bottles and selling flowers. My parents would give me spending money, but I was always wanting to buy more stuff from the five-and-dime store, candy, and pop. So, I developed a few entrepreneurial tricks to supplement my income.

The best gig was returning pop bottles to stores to collect the deposit paid when they were purchased. Recycling was a thing long ago. Housewives typically didn't want to drag the empties back to the store. I had a little red wagon and would make the neighborhood circuit, knocking on doors and asking if they had empty pop bottles. I remember one day, this one house had bottles stacked to what seemed to be the ceiling on their back porch. They must not have returned them for a year, or they had a huge party. I was going to be rich, this required multiple trips to the grocery store that was 3 blocks away. The clerks were giving me a look like I stole them or something, but I didn't care since I had candy and pop money burning a hole in my pocket for weeks after that haul. My normal haul would be like 4 or 5 six packs of bottles at a time. I didn't take them to my corner grocery store because I could get double the return at the bigger grocery store a few blocks away. Besides, she was a grouchy old lady.

I had a short-lived gig selling flowers. When I was about five, we had a neighbor who had a lovely flower garden. I decided to sell handfuls of flowers that I picked from her bountiful garden. I would take a bunch of flowers, knock on a door, and ask for a nickel. A cute kid selling flowers for a nickel worked great until I knocked on the door of the neighbor who had raised the flowers. She immediately recognized that I was trying to sell her flowers. She flipped out and started yelling at me while marching me home yelling at my mother about what a rotten kid I was for mutilating her garden. Yep, that ended that plan.

Pop bottles were great year-round revenue, not seasonal like flowers.

Turner's Groucheria (Grocery)

The corner grocery store was operated by a mean old lady, Helen Turner. Everyone in the neighborhood said she was a grouch. When I was a kid, she was 'old", though she may have been only about 50. I always called it Turners Groucheria because she was so grouchy. She hated kids yet sold candy. It wasn't a large grocery store, maybe 1000 square feet, but she had some basics like soap, cigarettes, milk, bread, and a limited meat counter. My mother disliked her, so she sent me over occasionally with a note to buy a few things, this wasn't our main grocery store. I was my mother's emergency cigarette runner, "Marlboro's filtered in hard pack" said the 5 yr old to the clerk.

I remember going to get some sliced bologna and watching Helen operate that big stainless steel, dangerous-looking slicing machine. It had this huge razor-sharp spinning blade that terrified me. How did she not slice her hand off? I remember telling Helen 'I want a half pound sliced thin for fried bologna sandwiches. It was the kind of lunch meat that had this plastic rind that had to be taken off before it was fried for our sandwiches. We called them bologna cup sandwiches because the slices would curl up when it was fried. A great treat.

As I said earlier, Helen hated kids. Every time a kid entered the store, she would follow them around asking what they wanted. "Hurry up and get what you want and leave". And so, the battle began. Every year at Halloween, her windows would get soaped, and I mean heavily soaped so much she couldn't see out the windows. One year this escalated into her windows being paraffined. It looked the same as soap, but it can't simply be washed off. It had to be scraped off with razor blades.

So, the day after the paraffin incident, my mother needed something; when I entered the store, Helen immediately jumped into interrogation mode. 'Did you do this to my windows'? I said I was only five and couldn't reach that high, pointing to the upper windows. (I was tall enough to do the lower windows and helped the big kids.) She then asked me who did it. I told her I didn't know even though I was there with the entire gang. I knew the neighborhood code, 'snitches get stitches. She then got all nice with me offering me a free candy bar for information on the culprits… 'Was it Fred or Jeff or John or Phil??' I said I didn't know. She offered me even more candy, but I held firm.

Fred, Jeff, John, and Phil, all owe me big time for not confessing 65 years ago. I was no rat bastard. I need to collect my debt for not ratting them out. Please send me two Snickers' bars in a plain brown wrapped envelope.

Daredevil Bike Rider

Our neighborhood was a great place for kids to grow up, our parents all had the same free-range philosophy, 'Kids should play outside'. This led to many inventive events when left to our own creativity. My best friend Darryl's younger brother Ferrell was wild at times. His bike riding skills were tremendous, you might even say impressive. He was always building small ramps with boards and bricks to make jumps and doing very well. His bike would jump in the air maybe six inches or so, sometimes leaving skid marks upon landing. That was cool.

One day he decided to make the ramp of all ramps. He had found a large plywood board and gathered several cement cinder blocks to make what he called – 'Mega Super Stupendous' ramp. This ramp dwarfed the previous ramps by a factor of ten, it must have been two feet tall at the top of the ramp. His confidence was, shall we say - sky high. All the kids were gathering around to witness his record jump. It was going to be epic.

So many kids had gathered to see this event, and he decided at the last minute to add some additional excitement. He said he needed some kids to lie down behind the ramp, and he would jump over them, landing safely way past them. I volunteered immediately and grabbed a spot in front of the ramp. This vantage point would be a great viewing spot to eyewitness this record jump. I and two others volunteered, and it was time for the jump.

He went way down the sidewalk to be able to get enough speed to make the jump a success. There was a large crowd of kids screaming to cheer him on. I felt the electricity in the air, anticipating seeing his bike flying over me. What could go wrong?

I don't remember which adult came out of their house screaming 'Stop! You idiots are going to kill someone.' Looking back now as a rational adult, I still think he would have easily cleared us and landed safely.

Broken cookies

Linne's Bakery in our town had the best locally made baked goods, cakes, breads, donuts, eclairs, cookies etc. Even now, my mouth is watering after all these years just thinking about it. You could smell the place a block away. They had a huge front window so you could see the glass cases lined inside with all their great stuff. They always had a crowd in the store. It was in the center of town on the main street not far from my house.

Linne's Bakery

My buddies and I used to ride our bikes all over town on the sidewalks downtown despite numerous warnings and admonitions from pedestrians and shopkeepers. We knew bike riding in the busy streets was far more dangerous. Besides, we never knocked over any old ladies riding our bikes on the sidewalks. I was careful.

Most of the time we didn't have enough money to buy from the bakery but when we did it was always great to splurge on their donuts and eclairs. One day Darryl and I decided we wanted some great cookies from Linnes.

We parked our bikes out front and got into line. They always had a line out the door because their stuff was so good. Darryl and I finally got to the front of the line and we both took all our money out and put it on the counter. It was just a few pennies and maybe a nickel. We asked if that was enough to buy a couple of cookies. The lady behind the counter said no, it was not enough money. I got an idea about unsellable items they might have. So, I asked if they might have any broken cookies that might be cheaper, knowing they only sold the best-looking and best-tasting stuff. Nobody wanted broken cookies. The nice lady said they did have a few broken and yes, they were cheaper. I watched her grab some unbroken cookies from the case and break them before putting them in a bag. I guess we looked like poor waifs who hadn't eaten in a week and needed a handout. Whatever she thought, Darryl and I got our cookies. It didn't matter to us whether they were broken or not.

Darryl and I tried this scam a few more times but it never worked again.

Halloween Costume

I loved watching old horror movies on Friday's late night TV shows that my parents let me stay up to see. Our local TV station had a late-night host named Selwin whose persona included pasty pallor, upswept eyebrows, sunken cheeks, long sideburns, a black cape, and a broad-brimmed hat. His show was on channel 8 every Friday night where he would introduce movies plus cut in with acts, bits, and comments prior to commercial breaks. Selwin's lead-in line was "It's Fright Night on Channel 8" and he would close each show with "Good night. . whatever you are". I loved any movie Boris Karloff was in, I especially enjoyed being scared by the 1932 Mummy movie starring Boris. I was fascinated by the gauze that they had wrapped the mummy with to preserve him for 4000 years. It is said that during the cycle of the full moon, the fluid from the brew of three tana leaves was to be administered to the creature to keep him alive. Should despoilers enter the tomb of the Princess, a fluid of nine leaves will restore movement to the monster. Great stuff, I loved that genre of movie even at 9 years old.

Selwin

I talked my mom into letting me go to school for the Halloween costume party in a homemade costume, the plan was to be wrapped in gauze like the Mummy. Every year the entire school in costume would parade around the playground before going downtown so the merchants could see the kids. There was also a prize for the best costume. I was positive my idea was a winner, so much better than buying a stupid plastic mask. I was always sure my ideas for these school contests were surefire winners. Mom went to several stores and bought many rolls of gauze. When I left home "I Was the Mummy" or a horrific burn victim.

My head was wrapped with a little area for my eyes and mouth open. Either way I was positive I would win the grand prize. Boris Karloff would have been so proud. I had to walk 3 or 4 blocks to school and then sit in class for a while. As time wore on my costume slowly started to unravel. As best a 9-year-old could do, I tucked here, I rewound there. The more I fidgeted and squirmed, the more gauze came loose. I was dragging around half my costume by the time of the parade. I had a great teacher that year, Mrs. McDonald, she would often see me around town when I was an adult and give my check a pinch. She saw I was clearly in distress, nearly in tears, and suggested I just stand with her and the other teachers to watch the parade. I knew my costume had failed and the prize was lost to some twerp with a store-bought face mask. I still think my idea was a winner, it was the execution of the plan that fell short. A few more tana leaves boiled was all I needed.

Piano Lessons and Singing

Some people were graced with the talent to entertain us musically, I learned early on that my musical talents were extremely limited and my contribution to the world of music would be that of audience participation. I truly do enjoy watching other people entertain. I think it was when I was about ten that I got my first

"Jerry Lee Lewis" Young

dose of reality. My parents bought an upright piano and told me they had lessons arranged for me. This lady was well known in the community, having taught hundreds and hundreds of youngsters for decades. I was truly excited about the possibilities. My first lesson went well I thought, she said the key to learning to play the piano was practice and more practice. I can't remember the two songs she assigned but I dutifully played them day and night. I can still find the middle C on the keyboard. In the next lesson, she worked with me on playing with a sense of rhythm. Apparently, this was not something I was born with. She assigned two more new songs and told me to practice as much as possible. By my fourth lesson, I remember after my lesson, the teacher waved to my mom sitting in the car to come inside. She told me I could go, and she wanted to talk to my mom alone. Oh Boy, I was getting some special praise on how well I was progressing. When my mom came back to the car I asked about the meeting. She said I wouldn't be going back for any more lessons. What! I was going to be the next Victor Borge or, at least, Jerry Lee Lewis. I did everything this nice lady told me and now I am not going back. I later overheard my mom talking to Dad. She told him the piano teacher said there was no need to torture me and everyone else with more lessons. They both agreed my practice was torture to them. Oh well, I guess I will just become an athlete.

My second dose of reality came when I was in the fifth grade. I had moved to a new school, and my new music teacher lived next to my grandparents, so I had known her since I was a toddler. The annual school musical was in the works, and I was hoping for a lead role. My grandmother volunteered to sew costumes, so how could I not get a lead role? Our teacher announced the cast for the play, and I didn't get any lead parts. I was in the chorus as a pirate. We had one song and a short dance. I thought OK, I would be the best dang pirate she ever had in a play. I learned my singing lines and practiced my little dance faithfully.

Putting them together was a little struggle. I decided I needed to really belt out the words since we were singing in front of the entire school and parents in the gym. We had a couple of rehearsals, and I really was projecting my voice out there. I had this role nailed. It was the day of the performance; I was wearing my pirate costume sewn by my grandmother. It was show time. The moment was nearing when the pirates were to take the stage. The teacher, whom I had known most of my life, pulled me aside and whispered in my ear. "George, don't sing the words, just mouth them"

WHAT? I was crushed. I got so upset that I messed up my little dance moves and sent us pirates crashing into each other. Lots of chuckles were heard from the audience, I am sure it looked cute, but I was dying on stage.

How bad could my singing have been for a 5th-grade play to instruct me NOT to sing? Message received loud and clear. First, my piano teacher and second, the 5th-grade music teacher gave me the message that I was not cut out for the performance side of music. Now I didn't have to worry about music cluttering up my development path to adulthood I could concentrate on other 'stuff'.

Parent meeting with the principal

We moved when I was in the fifth grade from my old neighborhood in the city to a brand-new house that my parents built in a new suburban subdivision. The city was growing, and the old schools were overcrowded. This meant a new school had to be built. In the sixth grade, I was in the first group of kids going to this new school. On the first day of school, the construction workers were still putting the final touches on the building, but we were thrilled with the new school. My teacher, Mr. Drake, was also the principal and coordinator for construction details. This all meant occasionally we would get extra-long recesses when he had meetings to deal with stuff. Some days, he would skip our recess, telling us he was preparing us for the seventh grade when there was NO RECESS.

Overall, he was a terrific teacher, he was also our basketball coach. I loved basketball. We had a backboard with a rim installed at our new house, and I shot hoops day and night. We had some flood lights shining on the driveway/basketball court, I was going to be the best Hoosier basketball star even if I didn't have time to do my homework. This brings us to a special meeting my new teacher/principal/coach requested with my parents and me.

Oh Boy, he wants to update my parents on my excellent school year. Well, I couldn't have been more wrong. The meeting was scheduled for after school and no one was in the classroom. He had three desks set up in a semicircle surrounding the desk he asked me to sit in. He sat in the chair directly in front of me and my parents flanked him. I started to get the feeling this wasn't the meeting I had envisioned. I don't remember his exact words, but it boiled down to 'George is not performing up to his potential, he could be an A student like his friend Cydney'. I am still friends with her to this day, she was always a top performer in everything she did. Clearly, I needed an excuse to get out of this mess, so I threw her under the bus.

I blurted out, "But Cydney cheats". My parents were friends with her parents, they looked shocked. My teacher was slack-jawed and said, "What in the world are you talking about. Cydney is above reproach". He said, "Young man, you better explain yourself; she would never cheat."

So I now had to explain how she had been cheating. I said, "Cydney cheats by studying in the evening and memorizing stuff in the books". I felt it was more of an educational achievement just to use my innate abilities and God-given knowledge. I was ok with mediocre grades because it reflected my true intellect, not some artificially boosted effect of studying. And besides, I didn't have time to study because I needed to practice my hoops in the evening. I can still see my teacher's face as he did a double-palm smash on his forehead and sighed deeply. My parents were in shock. I don't think this meeting designed to boost my educational productivity was going in the direction they all had hoped.

I then had to listen to this long explanation about studying was not cheating but the best method of learning. My NBA career was put on hold when the teacher/principal/coach told me I wasn't very good at basketball. He used an analogy that studying was like practicing jump shots. I responded that I practice jump shots all the time, and you just said I was not very good, so how is studying going to improve my grades? Despite having a great argument, my hoops time was shut down until my grades improved. My teacher and parents agreed I would get a weekly progress report instead of the normal quarterly report card. I started bringing home my books with the best intention of cheating to improve my grades. My parents gave me a lot of micro supervision, and slowly, my grades rose from mediocre to so-so to OK. I never had the drive to achieve perfection in education. I learned later in college that I needed to learn some study skills and habits quickly, or I was shipping off to Vietnam. That's all I really needed, some serious motivation. Unfortunately, at that point in my young life, neither my parents nor Mr. Drake had a big enough stick.

Mother

My mother, Virginia Moore Young, was our family's disciplinarian despite her diminutive frame of 5ft and 100lbs. She never hesitated to dispense immediate punishment with whatever was within reach; a wooden spoon, flyswatter, yardstick, magazine etc, etc. I can't say I didn't deserve it; I think I was eight before I learned my name wasn't really "GEORGEGODDAMITSTOPTHAT"

I remember once right after I had my teenage growth spurt when she was yelling at me for some long-forgotten indiscretion of a brain-dead teenage boy when she was yelling at me in the kitchen. Maybe I was caught drinking milk straight out of the carton??

I was towering over her by a full foot while she was giving me a dressing down. She suddenly grabbed the back of her neck in pain as she was bent in a very awkward position pointing her finger in my face.

I said, "Hold on for a second, Mom, hold that thought," and I went to the dining room and brought a chair into the kitchen. I held out my hand to help her climb onto the chair so she could be in a position of power over me. She burst into laughter and could not regain her composure nor even remember what I had done. Thanks, Mom, for everything.

Pink Tighty Whities

My mother taught me a lot of household chores as I was growing up. I was her sous chef during fancy meal productions and still enjoy cooking. I appreciate all the lessons learned, well maybe not the part about cleaning the toilet. One thing she would NOT pass on her wisdom to me was laundry. She would not let anyone near that process from gathering, washing, drying, ironing, folding, or putting away said objects. Clean neatly ironed clothes just appeared in my dresser at home. I was sent off to college with zero knowledge about those procedures. In about week three of dorm living, I noticed my clothes were not magically appearing in my closet; they were clean, fresh-smelling, and ready to wear. After some inquiries with other troglodyte dorm dwellers, I was informed about this room in the basement called the 'laundry room'. I was told you needed lots of coins and detergent to make this chore easy.

I had a large orange laundry bag made from parachute material that my mother included in my freshman leaving home package. Being out of clean clothes meant stuffing everything I had into that bag to begin my trek to the basement. I had purchased one new item of clothing when I hit the Indiana University campus, the requisite Crimson Hoosier sweatshirt. Having worn that many times, it had a noticeable funk and was included in the laundry bag.

I descended into the dank basement, where these machines were reported to be ready to do the magic cleaning process. The coin-op machine to sell detergent was easy. I got several boxes of the powder, pulled clothes out of the parachute bag, and stuffed them in the washer. I soon noticed it was going to take two washers to fit all my clothes in even if I stuffed them tightly. I wasn't too sure how much soap to add but I sprinkled some on top of each load and added the required number of coins. The machine started its thing, and I went back to my room. A few hours later I went back down to put the clothes into the dryer and found my wet clothes lying on the floor. Evidently, you were supposed to hang out and move them immediately to a dryer so others could wash their clothes upon completion. Lesson One learned the hard way.

Lesson Two, also learned the hard way on my very first ever load of wash. Separate colors, especially the new crimson IU sweatshirt. I noticed my tighty whiteys were now very pink. I assumed the drying process would return them to the nice white color that I was used to wearing. When the dryers finished, I noticed the pink had not departed.

Yes, I was the only freshman boy in Wright Quadrangle to have pink tighty whities. MOMMIE!!!

Herman B. Wells

My first introduction to Chancellor Emeritus Wells was in 1968 at the Indiana University freshman orientation assembly in the large auditorium. Many speakers that morning told us about the University and life on campus. It was all a bit overwhelming coming from a small Hoosier town where everyone knew your family back in the 19th century. Herman Wells was the president of the university for 25 years from 1937 to 1962. As an 18-year-old freshman, he seemed ancient, but it turned out he was only 66 years old. I don't remember what the other speakers talked about, but I remember distinctly two things that Herman said. First, he told us to look to the left and to the right at the people sitting next to us. He said two of you won't be here in January for the beginning of the second semester. Second, he invited us to his house to meet his mother and have some ice cream. Holy Cow, this guy was older than Methuselah and we were getting to meet his mother. As I was leaving the auditorium, I ran into Darryl, my oldest friend since we were in diapers. He was living in another dorm near mine. We both were intrigued by the offer of free ice cream and the possibility of meeting some freshmen girls, so we planned to meet later.

Herman, as part of his retirement package, got a free house

across from the main library on campus, plus several live-in students to assist his needs around the house. Darryl and I arrived a little early. We didn't want to miss the ice cream. Just as we arrived two of Herman's house boys were carrying his mother out onto the lawn. She was seated in a high back winged chair, and they easily transported her and the chair to the end of the ice cream line. Our IU careers were off to a great start. We got to meet Methuselah's mother and had free ice cream on a hot September afternoon. Herman's parting words to us, "If you ever need anything, I am here to help you".

During my sophomore year, I had trouble with a marketing professor. I was going through the normal channels trying to meet the professor during his office hours with no success. I tried both the head of the Marketing department and the Dean of the Business school trying to resolve my issues with little success. I remembered that my newest friend Herman was once the head of the business school, so I made an appointment. I laid out my issues with the professor, and Herman agreed there was a problem. He said he would make contact and get this resolved. I was skeptical that in a large university, he would get to the bottom of the problem. True to his word, Herman Wells was there 'to help the students'. I am glad I went for the free ice cream.

Chancellor Emeritus Wells remained in this role until his death in 2000.

I will not talk in class

My third-grade teacher at Charles Major School, Mrs. McDonald, was a great teacher. I enjoyed being in her class, maybe I enjoyed it a little too much. I was getting in trouble talking too much with my fellow classmates. She gave me an extracurricular assignment to try to curtail my exuberance. My charge was to write in my best printing 'I WILL NOT TALK IN CLASS ANYMORE' (100) one hundred times. This punishment seemed excessive to me, and it threw my inventive brain into overdrive to figure a way around this undertaking.

Finally, I had a plan to reduce the repetitive nature of this punishment. All I had to do was tie 5 pencils together and the number of times would be reduced a lot. This workaround plan, when you think about it, was actually not cheating but helping my math skills. To get 100 sentences, I only needed to write it 20 times. That was my plan, and I was going to stick to it. After many failures getting the pencils lashed together properly spaced and angled, I finally went into production. The final product looked like crap, the pressure wasn't even and the paper tore in places, but it was done, written 100 times. Mrs. McDonald apparently didn't like my inventiveness and creativity. She not only told me I had to do it over but sent home a note to my parents.

I got in trouble at home and now had to re-do it. All that engineering time was wasted. My brain was still trying to figure out a way to reduce the time. I decided I could write the words one at a time down the sheet in a column rather than write each sentence one at a time. I, I, I, I, I you get the idea. My end product again looked horrible and probably in reality was not any faster. Mrs. McDonald knew exactly what I had done when I turned it into her. She must have been a teacher for a long time to see through my plan. Another note home with instructions to increase the punishment to 200 times. Arrghh This was not going in the direction I wanted. I got grounded at home until I finished my assignment written nicely.

As an adult I would occasionally run into Mrs. McDonald

around town and she always would grab me by the cheek and say "Georgie, how are your sentences coming along". The woman never forgot anything.

Mrs. Crabby Appleton

My mother volunteered to be a room mother for a couple of years in my early grade school years. Room Mothers provided much-needed assistance to the teachers, bringing cupcakes and cookies for special celebrations like classroom parties and holiday events. I am sure there were other duties but that is the part I remember. It was very cool to see the other kids get excited when my mom came into the room with snacks. I always felt very proud. My first-grade teacher, Mrs. McNamara was a gem, the perfect teacher to gently start my education process. I don't remember any incidents when my mom was room mother that year. My second-grade teacher, Mrs. Lane, was not a smiling, friendly teacher. Perhaps I was spoiled from having such a great first-grade experience, but I always thought Mrs. Lane was downright mean and dour.

Before school each day I got to watch the Captain Kangaroo show. One of the features of Captain Kangaroo was a very simple 5-minute-long hand-drawn animation called Tom Terrific. Tom Terrific and his Mighty Manfred, the Wonder Dog were the main characters, always having great adventures. I watched this cartoon very intently and got into a side character, an arch-foe of Tom Terrific named Crabby Appleton, whose motto was, "I'm rotten to the core!" Crabby Appleton was the meanest villain that ever 'villed'.

As I was leaving the house for school, I would announce that I was going to go see Mrs. Crabby Appleton, rotten to the core, the nickname I'd given Mrs. Lane. My mother and little siblings would wave goodbye to me, wishing me good luck with Mrs. Crabby Appleton.

I can't remember which holiday it was, but I remember being excited because my mom was coming that day to be room mom with treats for all my classmates. The neighbor that was going to babysit my little brother and sister fell through so Mom had to bring them in tow. I suddenly was very apprehensive but had no clue to the danger that was about to unfold.

My teacher, Mrs. Crabby Appleton, I mean Mrs. Lane asked me to come up front and introduce my mother and siblings to her and the class. So, I got up and was introducing my siblings to my teacher when my 3-year-old brother blurted out "IS SHE MRS CRABBY APPLETON?" My 2-year-old sister then started parroting what he said while my mother was desperately trying to shush them both. My teacher was asking me who this Mrs. Crabby Appleton person is. I was mumbling something about Captain Kangaroo and just went to sit down. The whole class was laughing since they also watched Captain Kangaroo before school. I was so embarrassed.

It was like Art Linkletter show where "Kids Say the Darndest Things", but I am sure my mom was even more mortified than me.

Childhood House

I have lots of great memories of the house 106 St Mary Street, it is the first house I remember living in. It was a two-story American Foursquare house built in 1905. It basically was a big square box. The staircase leading to the upstairs was the quarter turn style, which had a 90-degree turn and a landing part way down. My bedroom was at the top of the stairs. The staircase led down to the living room where our TV was located.

Stairway

I used to sneak partway down the stairs at night after I was supposed to be in bed so I could listen to the TV shows. I wouldn't go past the landing because the parental units could see me if I stayed on the upper section I could not be seen. The only disadvantage I could see was only listening to the TV; I couldn't see the screen. Frequently, I would fall asleep on the stairs, and my parents would find me lying on the stairs with a pillow.

The stairwell had a railing with newel posts and custom-turned balusters. I remember one night when listening to the TV show wasn't enough. I just had to see what was going on the screen. Trying to look at the TV with my head pressed against the balusters was tough. I decided I would squeeze my head through the balusters. It was a tight fit, but I successfully pushed my head through and was able to see the TV just fine. I made some sort of noise; I can't remember if it was a sneeze or cough, but my parents turned around and saw me. Yikes, they yelled at me to get back in bed or get a spanking. I tried to pull my head back between the balusters but couldn't. I was stuck, I mean I was really wedged tight.

Finally, my parents believed that I could not get my ass back in bed. They came to help extract me from the stair railing. One parent pulling and the other pushing was about to rip my ears off. All the commotion woke my younger siblings and quite the scene was developing. They decided I got through there, and my head must have swollen, so they needed to find a solution. First, they tried greasing my head, I think they used a tub of Crisco from the kitchen. That didn't work, but my whole head and the stairs were now covered in that stuff. It was getting late, and the babies were screaming. The situation called for desperate measures. My father was not a handyman by any means. He had very limited carpentry skills, but he rounded up a hammer and saw, swearing he was going to get my head out of the railing one way of the other. I thought he was going to saw my head off!!

It turns out he was going to remove one of the balusters. It was no easy feat for an unskilled craftsman, but he pounded on the baluster despite my head being just inches away. I could feel every hammer blow. I was starting to regret my decision to defy my parents and watch that TV show. I can't even remember what show it was. Finally, the baluster splintered enough they could pull me out. A quick shampoo of my greasy head and many promises to never do anything as stupid as that again, it was time to get some sleep.

As I mentioned, my father was not the handyman type, and that missing baluster remained missing until they sold the house. This was not an off-the-shelf baluster, so finding a replacement would have been tough. I wonder if families that lived there later ever wondered why some idiot would remove one of the balusters. Surely building codes would not allow this gaping hole.

Replacement Balusters

I recently sent a picture of the staircase from an old 1950s photo album to the home's current owner, asking what they knew, if anything, about the missing balusters. The reply I got back left me gobsmacked. The balusters and all the woodwork in the house had been painstakingly stripped of all the white paint. I bet the paint was lead-based, and that would explain a lot. Evidence showed that three replacement balusters had been custom made on the banister. These stick out from the rest because the top and bottom of the baluster have slightly different patterns. When these were installed, they somehow got installed upside down. If you look very closely you can still see the evidence of my head getting stuck over 65 years later. (See photo, Thanks Murielle)

My ears still stick out a little from all the pulling they did try to remove me. Although it was not quite as dangerous as Baby Jessica stuck in that well, back in 1987, I felt I was in a very perilous predicament.

Conclusion

They say one way to begin your conclusion is to make a reference to something you outlined in your introduction. I provided you with many confessions about my free-range anecdotes in my youth before seemingly reaching adulthood. My being is not just a series of screwups and misadventures, but that of a typical normal kid. Yes, some weird stuff happened along my path, but I also did lots of ordinary stuff.

I went to the swimming pool to hang around with friends and meet new acquaintances. After the pool, we would all go across the street to a White Castle hamburger knockoff for sliders. It was called the Nickle Nook, and yes you could get a hamburger for five cents. Maybe the board of health should have closed this place, but we all survived.

My bicycle gave me lots of freedom to explore all the great parts of my little town of 15,000 people and a few not-so-great parts. The city's terrific parks department provided structured adult-supervised summer activities. I could roam from one park to another in 15 to 20 minutes on my bike to play shuffleboard, weave a potholder, or just play in the jungle gym with other kids. I used to soup up my bike by attaching playing cards and sticking in the spokes with clothes pins, it made a cool motorcycle sound but also made my mom really mad when I used her good bridge cards. It was easy to find pickup games of baseball or basketball. My buddies had beanshooters, basically plastic straws that we could blow (white beans) projectiles. We would set up ambushes in alleys for other kids riding through our neighborhood, thus setting up long-standing rivalries. I still think those kids from Sunset were punks and deserved it. My wife claims bean shooters attacked her and her friends on their way to the city pool, but I have always denied it was me. Besides she kept taking the same route to the pool.

I went to the Boys Club in the winter to shoot hoops and play pool. They had an NRA program to teach proper gun safety and learn how to shoot properly. That was before it became a political monster. Ken and Swifty, the guys that ran that place, were legends to our generation. One day they would ban rowdy kids for life and then let them back in the following week.

In the summer we played hide & go seek a lot of the evenings. I can still hear Darryl shouting "olly olly oxen free". Everyone kept empty mayonnaise jars with nail holes punched in the lids for us to catch lightning bugs (aka fireflies). We put grass in the jars, so they had a place to hang out and the holes let them breathe. These jars then made great night lights to put in our rooms. The bugs would all synch their blinking for a light show the rest of the night. Other summer nights when the city maintenance truck came around fogging with DDT to kill the mosquitoes, I would follow along right behind the truck right in the fog path on my bike. I can still remember that sickly sweet chemical smell. Wait a minute, that is not a thing normal people do. Maybe that toxic chemical exposure triggered some of my odd growing-up experiences. Maybe my parents didn't like me best. Maybe all these stories are just false memories caused by delayed neurotoxicity from DDT and the lead paint.

My point of all this is that I had a good time remembering these stories and hope you enjoyed reading them. I think I finally know what I want to be when I grow up.

So, while this narrative may pause here, it's not the final

chapter. There's more to uncover, more to experience, and more stories yet to be written.

This is not the end my friend.

The Strand Theatre

Shelbyville, Indiana

AUTHOR INFORMATION

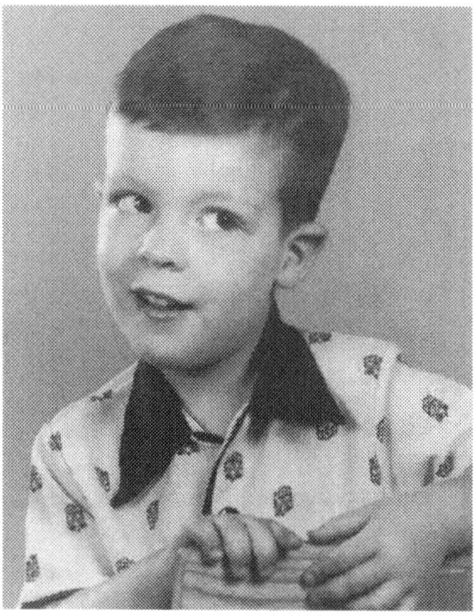

George Eric Young's family were Hoosier pioneers settling in Shelby Co, Indiana in 1822. He graduated from the Shelbyville Central school system before earning a Bachelor of Science in Economics followed by a Master of Business Administration from Indiana University, Bloomington. George worked in the distribution and sales of high-performance plastics for almost 45 years. His family moved to the PNW in 1985 where he, his high school sweetheart, two children, and three grandchildren still reside today. You can take the Hoosier out of Indiana but can't pull the roots out of the soul.

Front Cover Photo

This 1954 photo was taken in front of our house at 106 St Mary Street. In the background, you can see the corner of Franklin and St Mary, where Turner's Grocery was located. From an early age, my tricycle and, later, my trusty Schwinn bicycle enabled my exploration of my world.

That's How I Rolled

Made in the USA
Middletown, DE
06 January 2024

47202410R00104